THE ROLE OF LANGUAGE IN THE STRUGGLE FOR POWER AND LEGITIMACY IN AFRICA

THE ROLE OF LANGUAGE
IN THE STRUGGLE FOR POWER
AND LEGITIMACY IN AFRICA

Abiodun Goke-Pariola

African Studies
Volume 31

The Edwin Mellen Press
Lewiston/Queenston/Lampeter

Library of Congress Cataloging-in-Publication Data

Goke-Pariola, Abiodun.
   The role of language in the struggle for power and legitimacy in
Africa / Abiodun Goke-Pariola.
      p.   cm. -- (African studies ; v. 31)
   Includes bibliographical references and index.
   ISBN 0-7734-9351-4
   1. English language--Political aspects--Africa. 2. Language and
languages--Political aspects--Africa. 3. Africa--Politics and
government. 4. Language policy--Africa. 5. Africa--Languages.
I. Title. II. Series: African studies (Lewiston, N.Y.) ; v. 31.
PE3401.G65 1993
420'.96--dc20   93-30579
                                               CIP

This is volume 31 in the continuing series
African Studies
Volume 31 ISBN 0-7734-9351-4
AS Series ISBN 0-88946-175-9

A CIP catalog record for this book is available from the British Library.

All rights reserved. For information contact

The Edwin Mellen Press   The Edwin Mellen Press
Box 450   Box 67
Lewiston, New York   Queenston, Ontario
USA 14092   CANADA L0S 1L0

The Edwin Mellen Press, Ltd.
Lampeter, Dyfed, Wales
UNITED KINGDOM SA48 7DY

Printed in the United States of America

To my parents, Alphonsus Dada Pariola and Louisa Folasade Pariola, who inspired me by their own examples and ensured, against all odds, that all their children got the best education there is

CONTENTS

PREFACE

In February 1987, the Ife Social Sciences Forum assembled a group of people whose research interests were in African Studies at the Faculty of Social Sciences, University of Ife, Ile-Ife, Nigeria. The occasion was a workshop titled "Social Theory and African Reality," in honor of Professor Akinsola Akiwowo, foundation Professor of Sociology and Anthropology at Ife, who was retiring later that year. I was one of those invited to present a lead paper at the workshop. This book is the logical evolution of the issues I raised in that presentation.

I must acknowledge the profound influence of Professor Akinsola Akiwowo on this and other works of mine. My understanding of the thrust of Professor Akiwowo's work is in respect of his insistence on cultural and intellectual authenticity in the analysis and interpretation of the African social reality. This is a demand for the understanding of African reality as one peopled and fashioned by Africans, and one to be interpreted using indigenous African, as opposed to perhaps a Western--or Eastern--set of parameters or social-anthropological categories. A social theory of African reality based on a false sense of universalism in the sensibilities of human beings and the instruments of intellectual culture and discourse cannot but lead to a misinterpretation of our own reality.

My interests have subsequently developed beyond the simple question of language and social reality. For that would have limited me to issues of language, ideology, and reality, excluding the very important, and perhaps ultimate, question of power. Therefore, in this volume, I have attempted to look not only at how our choice of a medium of intellectual discourse influences our analysis of African social reality, but also how the erstwhile (European) languages of colonial domination continue to influence the contemporary and future African social reality that social scientists seek to describe. It also became obvious to me that I had to deal in detail with the appropriation of language into the struggle for power and legitimacy by elite groups in Africa, otherwise called state-building and language planning. Although I have used Nigeria as a principal illustrative case, I have also placed my discussion within an overall African context, especially drawing upon the unique, and often contrasting examples of Tanzania and the Republic of South Africa.

If at times the following discussion tends towards advocacy of some sort, I offer no apologies. It is a consequence of the ideological orientation of the discourse here, a conscious rejection of what Mazrui (1978) describes as the tendency in the dominant Western European tradition to believe that to be scholarly and scientific is to be intellectually detached and socially disengaged. After all, as any good Yoruba knows, the mind is located in the heart, which is the controlling center for all feelings and thoughts.

A modest faculty research grant from Georgia Southern University, Statesboro, Georgia, enabled me to travel to Nigeria to do archival research in the summer of 1989. This, coupled with the generous support of my chair, Jim Nichols, and my department, in the form of release time to do my writing have contributed in no small measure to the success of this project.

I would also like to acknowledge the support and encouragement of several friends and colleagues: *Baba* Akiwowo, who opened my eyes to a world I should have known about but did not; my *uncles* and senior colleagues, Sope Oyelaran and Rowland Abiodun, who generously shared their wealth of experience and knowledge with me; Talbot J. Taylor of the College of William and Mary, Williamsburg, Virginia, who read an earlier draft of the book and make several invaluable suggestions for improvement; Rohan Quince and Ayo Banji, who willingly assisted me in collecting data; my friends, Jide and Taiwo Owoeye and Chuck and Thelma Mike, who put me up while I did my field work in Nigeria; my other friends, Dupe Akin-Deko, Fred Richter, Pamela and John Rooks, Supo Laosebikan, Olumide Osinubi, Al Young, Francois Manchuelle, and Cliff Welch, who not only provided constant intellectual stimulation, but also never failed to give me moral support.

Finally, I would like to thank my wife, Adefunke, and my children, Wuraola, Olamide, and Folajimi, who put up with the countless hours I spent at the computer and always kept me in good humor. Needless to say, whatever shortcomings there are in this work are but mine alone.

ACKNOWLEDGMENTS

Alatas, S. H. From *The Myth of the Lazy Native*. Copyright © 1977 by Syed Hussein Alatas. Used by permission of the publisher, Frank Cass & Co. Ltd.

Barnard F. M. From *Herder on Social and Political Thought*. Translated and edited by F. M. Barnard. Copyright © 1969 by Cambridge University Press. Used by permission of the publisher, Cambridge University Press.

Cameron D. From *Ideologies of Language* by John E. Joseph & Talbot J. Taylor (eds.). Copyright © 1990 by John E. Joseph and Talbot J. Taylor. Used by permission of the publisher, Routledge.

Hawkes, T. From *Structuralism and Semiotics* by T. Hawkes. Copyright © 1977 by T. Hawkes. Reprinted by permission of the publisher, Routledge, New York and London.

Herder J. G. Excerpt from "Essay on the Origin of Language" from *Herder on Social and Political Thought*. Translated and edited by F. M. Barnard. Copyright © 1969 by Cambridge University Press. Used by permission of the publisher, Cambridge University Press.

Idowu, Bolaji. From *African Traditional Religion* by Bolaji E. Idowu. Copyright © 1975 by Orbis Books. Used by permission of the publisher, Orbis Books.

Joseph, J. E. & T. J. Taylor. From *Ideologies of Language* by John E. Joseph & Talbot J. Taylor (eds.). Copyright © 1990 by John E. Joseph and Talbot J. Taylor. Reprinted by permission of the publisher, Routledge, New York and London.

Laitin, D. D. From *Language Repertoires and State Construction in Africa* by David D. Laitin. Copyright © 1992 by David D. Latin. Used by permission of the publisher, Cambridge University Press.

McCrum, R, W. Cran, & R. MacNeil. From *The Story of English* by Robert McCrum, William Cran & Robert MacNeil. Copyright © 1986 by Robert McCrum, William Cran, and Robert MacNeil. Used by permission of Viking Penguin, a division of Penguin Books USA Inc.

CHAPTER ONE

INTRODUCTION

A. Sociolinguistic Profile of African Nations

Virtually all aspects of intellectual endeavors in African universities suffer from intellectual bondage, or orphanage, to some external standards. What does it mean to suffer from ideological orphanage? Akinsola Akiwowo defines the condition thus:

> To be in intellectual bondage is to have the faculty by which a person, a group of persons, a social class, or a race, conceives and comprehends and orders realities, under the continual and unrelenting influence of another person, another group of persons, another social class, or another race. (1988: 12)

This intellectual orphanage of African academia has been an enduring problematic. (See, for example, Isichei 1987, Mazrui 1976, 1978, 1980, Chinweizu 1975, Chinweizu *et al* 1980, Usman 1974, and Ngugi wa Thiong'o 1986).

Given the wide range of academic backgrounds of the scholars cited above--from the disciplines of social anthropology, political science and history, to literature--it becomes obvious that the problem of intellectual bondage is indeed widespread. I intend to argue that this situation is created not only by the academic curricula, but also by the medium of intellectual discourse. Whether it is in the field of literature, sociology, psychology, medicine, economics, or political science, scholars ultimately deal with issues of social theory. And social theory is itself ultimately no more than a set of postulates about the cultural behavior of a social group. If this is true, then, language which is the principal vehicle of expressing culture assumes a remarkable significance.

It is principally via language that we grasp, conceptualize, and inherit reality across generations. Man is, indeed, the "symbol animal". For as Halliday (1978) has rightly noted, language is the medium through which a human being becomes a personality, in consequence of his membership of society and his occupancy of social roles. Our analysis of reality, which is necessary for the formulation of theories about our cultural behavior, cannot be complete without a proper, concomitant apprehension of the position of language as a form of cultural behavior. Specifically, it is necessary to understand the role which language choice and language use have played, and continue to play, in this process of intellectual, social, economic, and cultural bondage. To fully comprehend this phenomenon, we must first understand the dynamics of the interaction between language, power, and ideology in the specific historical context of Africa.

African nations today present us with a complex picture of language use. This is because virtually all the nations which constitute Africa today are colonial creations. Hence, the reality of these nations normally features a European language, such as English, French, or Portuguese, and a number of indigenous African languages. For example, in addition to English Nigeria's 80-100 million people speak as many as 400 other indigenous languages, each with a number of dialects which sometimes tend to become mutually unintelligible. This situation has led to the characterization of African countries as multilingual, multicultural, and multinationality nations.

Much of the scholarship on the contact between English, the dominant European language, and African languages has been in the area of Applied Linguistics and language learning problems. Other areas of interest have been the description of emergent language forms, such as pidgins and creoles, and language planning issues. These are not only legitimate but very important issues for previously colonized and multilingual nations. It would seem, however, that the equally important and, perhaps more subtle, issue of language and social identity has been virtually ignored. This tradition of neglect is due in part to the fact that in most post-colonial African nations the use of metropolitan languages such as English and French has been taken as a *fait accompli*. And although their position as symbols and reminders of Africa's humiliating colonial experience has often led to calls for their rejection, their position as instruments of transforming the identity of Africans has received scant attention.

The few extensive studies which have raised questions somewhat similar to those addressed here have been carried out by political scientists (for example, Mazrui 1974, O'Barr & O'Barr 1976, and Laitin 1977, 1992). From a theoretical standpoint, the more interesting seem to be O'Barr & O'Barr (1976) and Laitin (1992). O'Barr & O'Barr's (1976) volume, *Language and Politics*, is a collection of essays which address the question of how varying linguistic environments may affect how the formal institutions of government. Tanzania, India, and New Guinea are used as case studies. Several of the articles address the specific questions of how language is employed by politicians and governments as a resource, and the impact of both monolingualism and multilingualism on state building. I will discuss some of their findings later as I examine language policies and language use in subsequent chapters.

In his book, *Language Repertoires and State Construction in Africa*, David Laitin uses game theory to project the future sociolinguistic outlines of African states. The basic question to which he seeks an answer is whether or not what he describes as Africa's "distinctive web of language use...[is] symptomatic of the early stage of state construction". If the answer is yes, then, according to him, the outcome of the present flux of language policies and language use will be "a rationalization of language use and agreement on a common language within [each] country's borders". If on the other hand African states demonstrate a unique case of state construction, then "political development will not lead to the one-state, one-language outcome typical of the idealized nation-state". His use of game theory to figure out language outcomes in African nations rests on a fundamental assumption that "society is often in disequilibrium and ...[that] the play of politics is usually about people, unhappy with the status quo, seeking to undermine apparent equilibria" (1992: x-xi), (and, presumably, seeking to impose a new one). The thesis he seeks to demonstrate is that language rationalization leading to monolingualism will be the exception in Africa, while a multilingual pattern of state building with a "3 $\pm$ 1 language outcome" (different from the Western examples of Switzerland, Belgium, and Canada) will be the norm.

Interesting and extremely valuable as these studies are, with respect to those issues which I intend to address here presently both are limited because they are principally interested in questions of state construction. This interest determines the questions that they have asked. As David Laitin himself admits in the preface to his volume,

> However great my commitment to speak to current issues in African affairs, this book was written primarily as a contribution to political science, through its use of game theory to analyze cultural politics and through its incorporation of historical variables to reveal distinct patterns of state construction. (1992: ix)

Far beyond examining the role of language in state construction in Africa, I am willing to delve into issues that "scientists" may consider treacherous, such as the relationship between language and social reality, as well as more mainstream issues like the role of language in negotiating power between individuals and groups.

Although it would seem today that many African leaders--with perhaps the notable exception of someone like Julius Nyerere of Tanzania--have settled for pragmatic policies which accord pride of place to European colonial languages, this has not always been the case. Indeed the apparently perfunctory calls for indigenous African official or national languages have historically been linked to the politics of nationalism in Africa as is the case elsewhere. For example, Jomo Kenyatta espoused the importance of Swahili in Kenya when at the end of a speech in English to the Kenyan Parliament in 1964, he decided to speak in Swahili, saying,

> I personally think that the time is not far away when we will be able to speak Kiswahili, which is our own language, in this House...
>
> Now that we have full independence we don't have to be slaves of foreign languages in our affairs, and consequently brothers, I wanted to make this point, because everything has to begin somewhere. If I had left this House without uttering a word of Kiswahili, I would have felt humiliated. (Quoted in Gorman 1970: 3)

While Julius Nyerere, in addition, emphasized the importance of Swahili for national unity in Tanzania (Polome 1980), seeking to promote Amharic, the late Emperor Haile Selassie of Ethiopia argued in support of "the growth and development of a national language [as] the prime foundation of the greatness of a[n Ethiopian] nation" (Taddese 1970, quoted in Laitin 1992: 92). In Morocco, King Hassan sought to reject the French heritage in 1958 by advocating an educational system which would be "Moroccan in thinking, Arabic in its language, and Muslim in its spirit" (Quoted in Sirles 1985: 69). And as Laitin (1992) correctly points out, today, many African intellectuals--for example, Ngugi wa Thiong'o (1986) and Nodolo (1989)--do believe that African cultural independence is indeed contingent upon the adoption of indigenous languages for national communication. The sociolinguistic problems that confront several African states, in particular the problems of language and national identity, have been compounded by the pattern of colonial experience. This pattern reversed the usual order of the evolution of nation-states. According to Fishman (1968a), the sociocultural entity normally precedes the formation of the geo-political entity. A homogenous sociolinguistic group may expand its territory through conquest and swallow up other ethno-linguistic groups. Over a period of time, the conquered may adopt the language and cultural norms of the conquerors, so that, eventually, the emergent nation would have passed through the stage of its consciousness as a sociocultural entity before becoming a geo-political one.

Indeed, pre-colonial African history may provide examples of Fishman's account of the historical process of language rationalization. Atkinson (1985) reports on such a situation in the spread of Luo in eighteenth century western Acholi. And, using Ambrose's (1982) study which relied principally on both linguistic and archaeological evidence, Laitin concludes that "the more centralized the political institutions,... the greater the spread of the language [of the dominant political group] among the progeny of nonspeakers" (1992: 83). Bird (1970) also provides similar evidence for the spread of Mandekan in West Africa. While the spread of Hausa in much of northern and Middle-Belt Nigeria may also be explained by similar factors, one can speculate upon what might have happened to those areas under the influence of the Yoruba Oyo Empire had it not disintegrated in the mid-nineteenth century. The fact that religious practices such as Ifa divination had already spread to places such as Dahomey, which at various times had been subjected to the empire's influence and control, would seem to point in that direction. In the light of such as examples as those given here, Laitin's conclusion that one may hypothesize that "precolonial African states, to the extent that there was centralized administration, induced the population living within their boundaries to learn the language of the central court" (1992: 83) seems plausible. In African countries such as Nigeria, nationhood was imposed at a time when no large aggregates had even achieved any strong sense of regional sociocultural identity. Thus, "Nation-building policies available to monarchs in the early modern period are not available to leaders of new states today" (Laitin 1992: xi).

Obviously, there exist significant gaps, not only in the amount of information available to us in the fields of African bilingualism and biculturalism, but more significantly in the area of social theory and cultural identity, as well as state construction. Yet, given the significance of language both as expression and embodiment of culture, as sociologists and political scientists theorize about African reality and the patterns of interaction between this part of the "Third World" and the rest of the world--the West, in particular--their analysis of contemporary African cultural behavior cannot be complete without a proper apprehension of the role that language has played, and continues to play, in the emergent African social reality. There is a pressing need to factor into our analyses the total sociolinguistic configuration of post colonial African societies: the emergence of language as "a tool of imperial design and colonial administrative convenience"; the use of language as "a tool for the preservation of the identity of ethnic/cultural minorities", to establish and maintain class advantages and class distinctions," and as a "tool of religious mobilization" (Bretton 1976).The existing gaps in scholarship may be filled by studies such as this, which fall within the larger area of political sociology.

B. Theoretical Considerations

The last statement above suggests that the present inquiry will straddle three basic areas of interest: politics, sociology, and language. Since we now have a professionalization of the academic role and an institutionalized differentiation of scholarly activities, it may be necessary to briefly reaffirm the link between these three. There is politics in virtually all social relations, even in the choice and use of language. Politics, after all, is really about the utilization and development of power. And since power is generated in almost every social group and institution, thus influencing virtually all social interactions, politics is indeed very pervasive in human society. This sociological tradition in politics is clearly reflected in the words of Harold Lasswell (1958) to the effect that "...the unifying frame of reference for the special student of politics is the rich and variable meaning of "influence and the influential," "power and the powerful"". This tradition understands power, just like authority and influence, as a characteristic social control process, not unique to any type of social group. Politics concerns the exercise of power in social situations, its structuring, as well as its legitimation within social groups.

Political sociology as a branch of sociology deals with power behavior in so far as it is relevant to understanding how political systems work. It is concerned with the issues of rule-making activities, that is, rules to govern particular self-contained units, and the question of social order.

From a narrow perspective, the political sociology of language will be concerned with the rule-making and rule-enforcing activities of sociolinguistic groups such as the speech community, and the various sub-units within it--the village, the family, the work place, etc. The questions will be : *Who speaks what language/dialect to whom, and when, and what are the consequences of breaking the sociolinguistic rules?* From a broader perspective, however, the political sociology of language will study the patterned co-variation of political and social behavior on the one hand, and language behavior and use on the other. It would address questions such as:

'what determines "the expressive resources available" in particular languages or to particular groups of speakers? Who or what *produces* "the conventions which apply to their use"?' how--that is to say, through what actual, concrete practices--is this done? (Cameron 1990: 88)

In other words, we will ask questions about how language may not only reflect social structures, but may also structure social reality, because "...language is not an organism or a passive reflection, but a social institution, deeply implicated in culture, in society, in political relations at every level" (Cameron 1990: 93). This study is largely influenced by the broader understanding of the political sociology of language.

Given the range of potential issues involved in a study such as this, the adoption of the multidisciplinary approach of political sociology is necessary. As Goody (1986) has rightly noted, "substantive problems are best dealt with not by one method or confining the discourse to one field, but by trying to pierce the heavy curtains of instituted and institutionalized boundaries and by drawing upon as wide a range of resources as are available" (vii).

C. Language and Power, Language and Ideology

In the preface to their book, *Ideologies of Language*, Joseph and Taylor (1990) make the claim that:

> Linguistic enquiry is inherently ideological; and the claims of scientific objectivity and autonomy themselves only function as component parts of the linguistic ideology dominant today.

Not only this institutionalized discourse is ideological; the very object of discourse itself is. In fact, that is a principal reason why the institutionalized discourse cannot be ideologically neutral. But what is perhaps rather surprising in the history of linguistics itself is that it is has taken so long for scholars to squarely address the ideological nature of linguistic inquiry. Some of the very earliest linguistic debates indeed clearly revealed this fact. For example, stripped of their elegant presentation, the very series of philosophical debates in Greek circles about "nature" versus "convention" represent some of the earliest recorded attempts at formally appropriating symbolic power. The ancient Greek philosophers pursued this goal in the debates whose stated purpose was to answer the question, *Is language governed by 'nature,' or by 'convention'?* To say that a particular institution was 'natural' was to imply that its origin lay in eternal and immutable principles. On the other hand, to say that 'convention' was the governing principle was to suggest that the institution had resulted from custom and tradition, and could therefore be changed. As the extreme "naturalists" like Cratylus whose views Plato reported in his dialogue *Cratylus* argued, *all words are indeed 'naturally' appropriate to the things they signify*. But, is this always evident to the ordinary folk? Of course not! It could, presumably, only be demonstrated by the philosopher who is able to discern the 'reality' which lay behind the appearance of things. Thus, *the power to know the true meaning of a word (language) gives the select few (the 'politically correct' philosophers) interpretive power which duly becomes a monopoly*. Thus, as Lyons (1968) explains, was born the practice of etymology, whose Greek stem--*etymo*--signifying 'true' or 'real' reveals its philosophical origin. *To lay bare the origin of a word and thereby its 'true' meaning is to reveal one of the truths of "nature"*. Thus, the philosopher as a member of an exclusive club acquires the power--*via language*--to reveal eternal truths.

The critical issues here are those of *language and power*, and *language and ideology*. Language is related to power in many different ways. Indeed, access to language is often a prerequisite to power, regardless of whether a social group is mono- or multilingual. Language varies in terms of dialects as well as individual competence in these varieties. And the relative status of dialects and, or, languages in communities indicates one way in which language serves as a marker or means of social power. For example, once upon a time in Europe, Latin was "the secret code of power", something outside the repertoire of the ordinary folk. Similarly, French once served as an instrument of exclusionary power at the German and Russian courts (Bretton 1976: 434). In contemporary Africa, the situation has been further complicated by the continuing presence not only of the erstwhile languages of colonial power, but also several indigenous African languages whose precolonial quest for hegemony have been revived, and which have subsequently entered into the fray.

Within many monolingual communities, access to a particular variety implies power. For example, Bernstein (1961) has drawn our attention to the existence of restricted and elaborated codes, manifesting social class and power differences in the use of English. (See also, Hess and Shipman 1965, Bee *et al.* 1969 and Feagans and Farran 1982). In this respect, the social stratification of language is the result of uneven distribution of cultural capital. We may also cite the example of the prestige difference between Standard American English and Black English in the United States of America. While there may be nothing inherently superior in the standard dialect of a language, it has prestige and power: people get away with many things simply because they possess it. The prestige and consequences of the possession of a standard dialect indeed constitute a good example of a socially constructed reality.

Furthermore, even within monolingual communities the social stratification of a society is indicated in the relative power of varieties of a language. This is in relation to the existence of diglossia, the stable and complementary existence of two varieties of the same language or two languages in a speech community (Ferguson 1959). Between the two, there exists a specialization of functions and domains. One, labeled H (High) is used for religious activities, letters, political speeches, lectures, news broadcasts, and newspaper editorials. The other, labeled L (Low), is used to give instructions to servants, waiters, workmen, in family conversations, and with friends. Such a distinction exists between Classical and Dialectal Arabic and French and Creole in Haiti. Indeed, the forms of diglossia are one way of realizing, linguistically, two complementary sets of values: *power and formality* on the one hand, and *solidarity and spontaneity* on the other.

In more recent times, several scholars, mainly in communication studies and pragmatics, have reopened the issues of language and power. (See, for example, Rommetveit 1968, 1972b, Kleiven 1973, Blakar 1973b, Blakar & Rommetveit 1971, 1975, Mueller 1973). The interest of most of these scholars, as stated by Blakar, is to avoid the pitfall of examining language "*in vacuo* or out of relevant contexts," and "without an explicit communication perspective" (Blakar 1979: 131-2). In other words, they insist that language must be studied within a social context.

In this context, power is used in the sense that anybody who is in a position to influence someone exerts power. Language may serve as a means of power in several different ways. There is, for example, the power of rhetoric, the ability to use language persuasively. Such was the skill that gave the Sophists their power in ancient Greece; it also gave sophistry a bad name. Poets and other writers may also derive influence from their awareness and exploitation of the power of words, while advertisers thrive on the manipulative power of language. Language also serves as means of power in the area of political propaganda, which Marcuse calls ideology (Marcuse 1968, 1969).

Although Marcuse uses "ideology" in the sense of "political propaganda", here the term has a wider reference, entailing the entire broad spectrum of human cultural behavior. Paul Roberge in his paraphrase of Moodie (1975) perhaps better expresses my use of ideology here. He describes ideology as "a set of articulations that derive from a system of beliefs and symbols embedded in popular consciousness, reinforced by civil ritual, and codified in the social order" (1990: 134). This understanding of ideology emphasizes the influence of civil religion, which he describes as denoting "the religious dimensions of the state...[and] is associated with the exercise of power and the 'constant regeneration of the social order'" (1990: 134), and the social philosophy--which defines "the units of social analysis (family, nation, social class, even mankind as a whole)--and the vesting of political power (in an individual, an ethnic group, a majority of individuals, and so on);" (1990: 135).

It is important to note that the power we exert as users of language need not be conscious or intentional. Indeed, quite often those who do, except if they are in a position of authority, do not realize that their simple choice of a language, or certain lexical items, gives them a concomitant power over others. Nevertheless, the fact remains that "The language user's social influence is...defined through effect or consequence, completely disregarding whether the effect is intended or not" (Blakar 1979: 134).

Language, it seems, may exert power and promote particular ideologies in at least three important ways. First, a speaker's linguistic choice "structures and influences the addressee's experience of the substance of communication". Second, the way a particular language conceptualizes reality influences those who acquire and use the language. That is to say, no language is ideologically neutral in respect of the human construction or interpretation of reality. Although this seems to take us back to the quagmire that was the Whorfian hypothesis, as I will demonstrate shortly, this is not really the case. Finally, given the fact that languages as dialects have varying status in any given community or context, the relative status of one also determines the relative status and power of a particular group (Blakar 1979). Language, then, indeed conditions us to cultural patterns because it serves as "an instrument of interpersonal behavior and...essentially a means of incorporating the individual into an existing cultural matrix and of guaranteeing his contribution to the needs and aspirations of the culture" (Lafall 1965: 24, 25).

Of interest to the specific sociolinguistic context with which I am concerned here are the second and third dimensions to language use and language processing. The third deals with language choice and power, while the second addresses the implications of the choices and use on our view of reality, in other words, the question of language and ideology. I have already briefly addressed the third issue and will postpone further discussion for now.

The debate over the relationship between language and ideology of course predates modern scholarship, involving not only linguists, but philosophers as well. Herder (1772), for example, was deeply impressed by the interconnection of language, culture, and community. So important to a community is their language that sociocultural entities only survived as such, that is, they maintain their identities only in so far as they succeeded in preserving their language as a collective inheritance. Barnard's summary of his views are particularly illuminating:

> Language [is] both the medium through which man becomes conscious of his inner self *and* [is] the key to the understanding of his outer relationships. It unites him with, but it also differentiates him from others. Imperceptibly it also links him with his past. By means of language he is able to enter into communion with the way of thinking and feeling of his progenitors, to take part as it were, in the workings of the ancestral mind. He, in turn, again by means of language, perpetuates and enriches the thoughts, feelings and prejudices of past generations for the benefit of posterity. In this way language embodies the living manifestation of historical continuity and the psychological matrix in which man's awareness of his distinctive social heritage is aroused and deepened. (1969: 22)

It seems that when we talk of language and ideology in the sense that Blakar and others, including Herder, do, we are back again to the question of language and reality. The literature is indeed replete with arguments that seek to prove the structure of the world on the basis of considerations about language. Most popular--and perhaps also most notorious--of these arguments has been the concept of *linguistic relativity*. The Sapir-Whorf hypothesis is so well-known that it needs little elaboration here. Simply put, based on their observations of different speech communities, the structuralist Sapir and his student, Whorf, concluded that these communities had different world views (Sapir 1931, 1949, Whorf 1956).

The question has been, if thought is tied to language, that is, the specific language that we speak, and if languages differ in significant ways, would not speakers of different languages then think differently? The answer may depend largely on how we see languages. Whereas scholars such as Chomsky are struck by the similarities between languages (language universals), others are impressed by the differences. For them, language is more than simply a neutral system of communication and thought: rather, to speak a particular language is "to adopt a parochial conception of reality" (Devitt and Sterelny 1987: 172). This is to be distinguished from the more radical concept that *reality itself*, and *not just how we think about*, or, *perceive* it, is relative to our language and culture.

The Sapir-Whorf hypothesis has been appropriately criticized. Its major shortcoming, as has been rightly noted by several scholars, is that it confuses *experience of the world* with *the world itself*. Even if it is true that we may consider language as "a classification and arrangement of the stream of sensory experience;" (Whorf 1956: 55), and also that "the world is presented in a kaleidoscopic flux of impressions which has to be organized by our minds--and this means largely by the linguistic system in our minds" (213), it does not logically follow that we should then leap to the admittedly attractive, but patently false, dramatic conclusion that "No two languages are ever sufficiently similar to be considered as representing the same reality" (Sapir 1949: 162).

This fault in logic seems to be a peculiar structuralist trade-mark. It is similar to the argument advanced by structuralist linguists as they reject reference and assert the absolute autonomy of language systems. In the process, they progress from talking about the language dependence of theories to the language-dependence of reality:

> since [language]...constitutes our characteristic means of encountering and of coping with the world beyond ourselves, then perhaps we can say that it constitutes the characteristic human structure. From there, it is only a small step to the argument that perhaps it also constitutes the characteristic structure of human reality. (Hawkes 1977: 28)

This structuralist relativism also argues that to change cultures, and therefore language systems, is to change worlds:

> all societies construct their *own realities* in accordance with mental or psychological principles that determine form and function...they covertly project these upon whatever the real world may in fact be...this is what *all* societies do, not just "primitive" or "savage" ones. (1977: 56)

Ironically, it is this alleged absolute autonomy of language which structuralist scholars use to argue for the independence of linguistic enquiry from issues concerning power and ideology. Whichever way we look at it, what language does is help us construct a theory of the world, and not the world itself. And this is the sense in which we are to understand the significance of the ideologies of language.

I have dealt at some length with the issue of language and reality and, in particular, the structuralist concepts of linguistic determinism because it seems to me to be the most obvious argument that might be marshaled against discussions of the effect of language on reality. I hope that the point has been sufficiently emphasized that the argument here is not about the dependence of reality on language, but rather that language as an embodiment of culture, transmits the ideological beliefs of those who possess a language.

Although Blakar and others have been more interested in ideology within a monolingual national context, I am more concerned here with the international dimension, since my sociolinguistic context involves languages across national boundaries. Nevertheless, Blakar makes what for the purposes of this study is one half of the critical point: getting one's labels for aspects of reality--particularly social reality--accepted represents quite an important act of social power. This is also the point which feminists make about language and ideology when they argue for the necessity of *engineering* language. As Julia Penelope argues, "English does more than hinder and hurt women: it proscribes the boundaries of the lives [they] might imagine and will [themselves] to live" (1990: xiv). While the syntax and semantics of English encode experiences of the world, she argues, the labels which have gained dominance indicate that these experiences are not those of women. This, it seems, is the kind of sociolinguistic status quo which Daniel Moynihan sought to legitimate when he wrote in a memorandum to the President of the United States in the turbulent sixties:

> what is at issue is the continued acceptance by the great mass of the
> people of the legitimacy and efficacy of the present arrangements of
> American society and of our process for changing those
> arrangements. (Quoted in Mueller 1973: 5)

Most significant in its ability to weave together these varying, and sometimes disparate, trends is the seminal work of the French sociologist, Pierre Bourdieu in his volume, *Language and Symbolic Power* (1991). Because of the importance of his articulation of his position and the centrality of his thoughts to the present volume, I will review his work at some length here.

Bourdieu sharply critiques structuralism and all forms of "semiotic" or "semiological" analysis which have been inspired by Saussarian linguistics. According to Bourdieu, both Ferdinand de Saussure (1974) in his use of *langue* and *parole*, and Noam Chomsky (1965) in his own use of *competence* and *performance* err in presupposing that language is an autonomous and homogeneous entity which is subject to a "purely linguistic analysis". This error, he argues, has led in linguistic and literary studies as well as in the social sciences to an exclusive reliance on the internal constitution of texts. In consequence, scholars beholden to this tradition tend to ignore the historical, social, and political conditions which determine both the generation and reception of their texts. Since language is not simply a means of communication, but rather also a medium of power, once we exclude the extra-linguistic character of speech, we lose a significant portion of the meaning of a linguistic exchange.

This philosophical orientation of structural linguistics as he describes it has important social consequences. For example, the belief in the autonomy of linguistics underlies the myth of the objectivity of linguistic inquiry. Hence Bourdieu's sharp criticism of the first assumption which underlies structuralism, an assumption he says is predicated upon an "intellectualist philosophy" which considers language to be no more than "an object of contemplation rather than as an instrument of action and power" (1991: 37). Blakar (1979) and Joseph and Taylor (1990) also make a similar observation.

While Saussarian linguistics may be said to exclude all inherent social variation in language (after all language is "a collective treasure shared by all members of the community") Chomsky's linguistics accords pride of place to the formal properties of language, ignoring the functional constraints on its use. It demonstrates a strong tendency to rely exclusively on just one of the factors involved in a linguistic exchange--a purely abstract linguistic competence thus denying the social conditioning of speech. Therefore, both Saussure's and Chomsky's grammars exclude the economic and social conditions of the acquisition of "legitimate" competence, as well as the constitution of the linguistic market in which this definition of the legitimate and illegitimate is established and imposed. In its apparent failure to comprehend the fact that "Grammar defines meaning only very partially...[and that] it is in relation to a market that the complete determination of the significance of discourse occurs", the formalist tradition in linguistics has not been able to escape its virtual reduction of the study of language to what would appear to be "a game devoid of consequences" (Thompson 1991: 38).

Of course, Bourdieu was neither the first nor was he alone in his criticism of the formalist tradition in linguistics. However, such criticism has generally come not from within "the house", but from scholars in the social sciences, principally sociologists and anthropologists. One of the earliest critics of Chomsky's extreme formalism was the ethnographer Dell Hymes (1977). But even his concept of *communicative competence* is presented as an "additional dimension" to the study of linguistic competence. Also, the field of sociolinguistics whose marginalization in mainstream linguistics further testifies to the continuing primacy of linguistic formalism displays a general tendency towards variations in accent or usage in a manner largely divorced from broader theoretical and explanatory concerns (Cameron 1990, Thompson 1991). Consistent and rigorous questioning of the fundamental assumptions of formal linguistics by scholars whose primary concerns are in language and linguistic studies have been rather recent. (See, for example, Joseph and Taylor 1990, Cameron 1990, and Thompson 1991).

What I find particularly remarkable about Bourdieu, beside the clarity and consistency of his criticism of the dominant tradition in language study, is the fact that he proposes a coherent alternative approach. He is not simply on a crusade to append "another dimension" to the study of language, but rather, having reached the conclusion that language is not ideologically neutral, he proposes a new basis for the understanding of language as a means of achieving symbolic power. As noted by Thompson in his introduction to Bourdieu's volume, rather than setting himself the goal of simply adding to the structuralist linguistic tools, he sets out

> To show that language itself is a social-historical phenomenon,
> that linguistic exchange is mundane, practical activity like many
> others, and that linguistic theories which ignore the social-
> historical and practical character of language do so at their own
> peril. (1991: 4)

Central to Bourdieu's theory are the concepts of *"habitus," "field"* *("market"* or *"game"), "capital,"* and *"bodily hexis".* *Habitus* generally refers to structured socially acquired sets of dispositions in any area of a person's life. It often governs our spontaneous reactions to various stimuli in the social environment. Bourdieu employs this and the other concepts in the general context of performance, and specifically also to linguistic exchanges by virtue of their definition as performances.

Bourdieu explains that *habitus* alone does not however determine behavior.

Behavior is governed by the interaction of *habitus* with *field*. The *field* or *market* is the specific structured space in which people interact. The nature of the interaction is further defined by the compendium of varying kinds of *capital* (economic, cultural, symbolic, etc.) which each of us as participants in a market have accumulated at any given point in time. In any given field, individuals struggle to maintain, or alter, the distribution of the various forms of capital which are specific to that field. In a sense, his ideas here bear some similarities to Laitin's description of the tension between "equilibria" and "disequilibrium" in society (1992: x-xi).

Specifically in the case of language use, we are to understand linguistic utterances as the product of the relation between a *linguistic habitus* and a *linguistic market*:

> Every speech act and, more generally, every action is a conjecture,
> an encounter between independent causal series. On the one hand,
> there are the socially constructed dispositions of the linguistic
> habitus, which imply a certain propensity to speak and to say
> determinate things (the expressive interest) and a certain capacity
> to speak, which involves both the linguistic capacity to generate an
> infinite number of grammatically correct discourses, and the social
> capacity to use this competence adequately in a determinate
> situation. On the other hand, there are the structures of the
> linguistic market which impose themselves as a system of specific
> sanctions and censorships. (Bourdieu 1991: 37)

This observation in fact forms the basis for the contention that language, and consequently linguistic inquiry, is never entirely self-contained nor neutral (Joseph and Taylor 1990). Even literary or artistic production or academic discourse that may at first seem to be "interest-free" are not: they are only more easily able to conceal the interests of their producers. To summarize Bourdieu's analysis of the way in which language relates to social life, first, language is not simply a means of communication, but is also a medium of power. Second, linguistic expressions are the product of the relationship between a *linguistic market* and a *linguistic habitus*. Third, individual choices are conditioned by the demands of the target social field/market (audience). Consequently, every linguistic interaction displays "the social structure that it both expresses and helps to create". I will return to

Bourdieu's sociology of language as I begin to analyze the sociolinguistic configurations of modern African societies.

Just as in Marcusian terms individuals in industrialized societies tend to identify themselves within the existing political structures and goals by accepting without question the social labels, those in developing "Third World" countries who acquire English as a Second Language (ESL) tend to do the same with the structuring of social reality as encoded in English. This also hold true for instances which involve other European languages. A principal means of ensuring the legitimacy of a given political order, such as for example, the "colonial world order" (See discussion on colonial capitalism in the next chapter) or the so-called "New World Order," is the transmission and regeneration of values which permit a limited degree of solidarity among members of the target political community. Dividing the linguistic capital and ideologies of colonized communities was one way this was done, and has continued to be maintained in Africa.

D. Focus and Scope of Study

At the beginning of his volume, *Language Repertoires and State Construction in Africa*, David Laitin asks why language outcomes matter, if indeed they do. The answer to the question, he claims, is multidimensional: it is at once psychological, economic, cultural, and political. The translation is that language outcomes matter because they are inherently matters of ideology and power. In writing this volume, I have defined for myself a fairly narrow theme in relation to the range of language issues one might examine in contemporary Africa. For one thing, I have limited myself to a study of the legacy of Euro-American colonialism in African societies. True enough, America was not party to the scramble for Africa. However, as any minimally perceptive observer of the economic, political and cultural scene in Africa--and indeed the entire world--today would concede, the economic, political, military, and cultural power of America has made that rather recent entrant into the world of imperial power play the dominant player and flag-bearer of Western ideology. Hence her inclusion in the consideration of external influences on the sociolinguistic configuration of contemporary African societies.

I intend to examine the significance of language in the process by which post-colonial African societies have been constructing their identities through a dynamic response to historical pressures. I will analyze the central role which language plays in the struggle for power and legitimacy between colonized Africans and the colonial powers, and how the inheritors of political power have used language not only as an instrument of state construction, but also to assert legitimacy. I will also address the important question of the emergence of language as an instrument in the negotiation of power between different groups of the elite class and ethnicities as well as by individuals in interpersonal relationships. The present volume will also speculate on how language choice and language use may help to define Africa's economic and political relationship with the rest of the world--in particular the Western world--as well as the apprehension of social reality by present and future generations of Africans.

In terms of coverage, I have chosen to use one principal illustrative case-- Nigeria--for my analysis and discussion of the complex interplay of language, power, and ideology in Africa. This is necessary not only to provide depth to this study, but also to avoid the conventional Western "wisdom" of often considering the entire continent of Africa as nothing more than a large country made up of different states. Also, some of the issues of ideology that I will address, especially in Chapter Six, specifically the question of language and social reality, can only be addressed meaningfully in the context of a culture of which the writer, following well-proven methods of anthropological studies, has been a primary participant.

However, having said that, African countries, among other things, share much in terms of recent historical experience. After all, the process by which modern African states have come into existence virtually all derive from a largely similar colonial experience. Thus, the discussion of Nigeria will be embedded within an expansive discussion of language and colonialism and post-colonialism generally in Africa as a whole. In particular, I will look at Tanzania and the Republic of South Africa in my discussion of language policy, state construction and group and state ideologies. There are not only significant divergences between these two countries and Nigeria in linguistic configurations, but also in ideological orientations. Both have significantly lower number of indigenous African languages (about 100 in Tanzania, and less than 100 in South Africa, in contrast to Nigeria's more than 400 languages). Also, while the Tanzanian sociolinguistic scene features a widespread African language, Swahili, in addition to the European language, English, South Africa features two European or "European-derived" languages--English and Afrikaans--which are virtually "African" by virtue of the significant settler and other mother tongue speakers in South Africa. These differences then offer us strikingly different, but sufficiently similar, contexts within which to examine the interplay of language and ideology and power.

Briefly restated, the object of the present enquiry is to seek an answer to the following question: *In the specific sociolinguistic context of Nigeria as a previously colonized African nation, how have the factors of language, power and ideology as explained above played themselves out?* Given the range of interest that I have specified, this volume will therefore address the interaction of the variables of language, power, and ideology in the process of state construction in Africa, as well as in group and interpersonal interaction and competition.

In terms of the cultural and psychological dimension to the construction of identity I will focus principally on the middle class, to the extent to which such a class can be identified in Nigeria and other African contexts. This middle class is the meeting ground as well as the major battleground for the power and ideological conflicts between European and African languages, between Western and African world views. Occupying a schizophrenic middle ground, the middle class is constructing its identity via a simultaneous rejection of the indigenous other and acceptance of the Western other. This process generates new cultural values in fashion, literature, religion, political consciousness, and a sharpening of gender contradiction.

Since the construction of identity is never a finished matter, identity, then, is in a state of perpetual flux, reflecting "the peculiar interests and values of individuals and groups at specific points in time". Since in the Nigerian context this class is still largely inchoate and ill-defined and also exercises considerable influence on the lower class, many of the observations made about it will apply to the generality of the population.

It needs to be emphasized that at issue here is not the entire question of the construction and deconstruction of identity in itself. I have limited myself to exploring the influence of language choice and language use on the emerging identity of a specific African society. And in view of the fact that the construction of identity in contemporary Africa cannot be divorced from the phenomenon of colonialism, a substantial portion of this study is in fact devoted to the linguistic dimension to the colonial experience in Africa. I will seek to answer the following specific questions: What is the role of language choice and language use in the establishment and definition of the power differential between the colonial powers and their African subjects in the colonial period, the inheritors of European power, the elite class, and the rest of society, individuals in inter-personal interaction, and groups competing for political power? Also, what are the implications of language choice and the dominant ideology of the English language and other European languages for the definition of the relationship between Nigeria and the outside world and the apprehension of social reality by present and future generations of Africans?

To bring these issues into focus, I will examine the linguistic response of the Westernized middle class to the colonial experience; analyze the political and educational language policies in post-independence Nigeria; assess the relative domain coverage of Nigeria's metropolitan language, English, and the indigenous languages since independence in 1960; and analyze the linguistic indices identified above both as causative and resultant factors in the emergent identity of the contemporary Westernized Nigerian elite as well as the generality of the people. As I have noted earlier in this section, I will look at the Nigerian situation within general context of Africa, paying particular attention to Tanzania and the Republic of South Africa, as appropriate.

CHAPTER TWO

LANGUAGE IN THE EVOLUTION OF THE COLONIAL NATION-STATE

A. Introduction

The colonial situation in Nigeria--as indeed was the case in other African countries--demonstrates quite clearly the nature of language as a critical tool in the acquisition and maintenance of power, as something capable of bestowing upon, or denying to the user, a great deal of symbolic profit, and by virtue of this fact, of affecting the construction of a society's social reality.

In this chapter, I intend to discuss the role of language in the imposition of colonial rule and the legitimation of power in Nigeria and other African societies. As I indicated in Chapter One, the colonial experience introduced new and more complex dimensions to the question of language and power in African societies. Principal among the ways in which was done was the topicalization of the issue of "national" and, or, "official" language(s). In this chapter, I will discuss the historical convergence of religious, economic, social and political factors in the process not only of imposing colonial rule, but of defining the relationship of language to power.

B. The Process of Colonization

In sub-Saharan Africa, the initial contact between Africans and Europeans, and indeed other foreigners, did not just begin in the 18th century. For example, as was the case in several other African countries, Islam had already established a foothold in parts of northern Nigeria. By the beginning of the 19th century, the kingdom of Borno to the north-east had already acquired the dubious distinction of being the main supplier of eunuchs to the courts of the Mediterranean Africa and the Levant. The first contact with Europeans had taken place four centuries earlier. By 1480, the Portuguese had begun conducting slave raids on the rivers west of the Niger Delta, exchanging their human booty for gold in modern-day Ghana. This is responsible for the name the Portuguese charts and other documents gave to the coastal region of Nigeria: "five slave rivers" (the Primeiro, the Benin River, the Escravos, the Forcados, and the Ramos) (Ryder 1969: 236). Obviously then, the first European language with which Nigerians came in contact was Portuguese. This fact is reflected in the strong presence of Portuguese in Nigerian Pidgin English. The English would not arrive for another century.

Given the facts above, why, we may ask, was the 19th century so significant? It is precisely because not until the 19th century did external relations begin to seriously threaten the traditional societies both politically or culturally. Before then, ideas and cultures had generally been borrowed and modified only after they had been tested and their relevance to the local interests and aspirations had been assessed. The English arrived in the second half of the 16th century, in search of ivory and pepper. By the 1630 and 40s, however, they had begun sugar colonies in the Caribbean, and this created their interest in slaves. Since the stakes were now much larger it also stimulated their territorial interests. The systematic invasion of the area known today as Nigeria by the English and the English language passed through three significant initial periods which ultimately set the stage for the eventual colonization of Nigeria and the imposition of English. First came the explorers, then the missionaries, and finally, the traders.

In spite of their avowed goals (The African Association, for example, was formed in 1788 to conduct "purely scientific exploration of Africa"), many explorers were clearly interested in the exploitation of the continent's resources, by force if necessary. The following quote attributed to Gerhard Rohlfs, a German explorer to the Middle-Belt in 1866, is illustrative of such other motives:

> May one of the Christian powers, using these advantages offered by
> nature, take possession of the Bauchi Plateau and colonize it with
> settlers from Europe under the protection of its arms! Here in the
> territory of the Hausa and Bolo Negroes, a great majority of whom

are still pagans, and who despise the rule of the Mohammaden Fulanis, a strong barrier should be established against the continued spread of Islam. Islam fills its confessors with heartless contempt of the infidel heathen, with fanatical hatred of Christians. It is Islam which causes the outrageous man-hunts among the Negroes; it is Islam which makes it difficult for European travellers to penetrate into the interior. (Rotberg 1970: 194)

Ideologically then, the explorers were by and large the *avant garde* of the missionary, the trader, and the soldier.

For several Christian missions--most of which had been founded in Europe and America towards the end of the 18th century--Nigeria proved a fertile ground for the gospel. The period between 1842 and 1892 witnessed the establishment of eight Christian missions in different parts of southern Nigeria. Despite the suspicion and hostility of some indigenous groups such as the Ijebu, for example, the missions continued to thrive. The Ijebu like the Edo, and rulers like Jaja of Opobo saw that the missionaries and their educated Nigerian cohorts were the harbingers of British colonization. The newly converted Nigerians were indeed often already spiritually and culturally lost. Samuel Ajayi Crowther, for example, received with great joy "the long wished for tidings"--the bombardment of Lagos by the British navy--"[with] *the destruction of Lagos, the stronghold and secure rest of the slave trade in the Bight of Benin...* The usurper fled into the bush...he has been a great plague to the whole nation...The English flag is now flying in Lagos" (Ayandele 1980: 375). To this, one can only add that it was not just the Union Jack but the English language as well that was flying high.

The traders were the last leg in the preparation for the colonization of Nigeria. The Royal Niger Company, for example, had its own armed forces and was in fact responsible for the colonization of several parts of Nigeria, just as was the case in Tanganyika (Tanzania) and the Belgian Congo (Zaire). Traders also often produced the final excuse, if any had been necessary, for the British to take over the land by force under the guise of "protecting British citizens and free trade".

In preparation for the eventual annexation of Nigeria, Britain had since the late 1800s embarked upon the process of neutralizing all visible African opposition to the institutionalization of British rule and the expansion and consolidation of

British central authority over the territory later known as Nigeria (Tamuno 1972). In May 1906 the Lagos Colony was amalgamated with the Protectorate of Southern Nigeria to form the New Colony and Protectorate of the Southern Nigeria and, in January 1914, the Amalgamation of the Southern and Northern Protectorates was effected, thus creating, at least on paper, the country of Nigeria.

C. Language, Education, and the Political Economy

To understand the rapid growth of the English language and, more importantly, its effects on the emergent Nigerian society, we must examine the introduction and the impact of Western education, of which English was the principal vehicle, on the colonial economy and the emerging Nigerian society. English was a principal tool in the imposition of colonial rule in Nigeria. One of the many ways in which it served this purpose was by its position as the language of the colonizer. That very fact carried with it considerable symbolic power. The relationship between the peoples of the country later known as Nigeria and the small number of British people in the political field became reflected in the linguistic market. Therefore, a study of language in colonial Nigeria is essentially a study of the progress of the English language, and the devaluation of indigenous languages.

Ever since the advent of the missionaries who preceded the actual colonists, the English language has been important in one sense or the other in Nigeria. Initially, its importance was somewhat similar to that of Arabic in the northern part of the country at the time the Islamic faith was introduced. It was the language of a supposedly superior race who had brought "religion and civilization". As the examination of the role of Arabic--the only other major rival to English in 19th century Nigeria--reveals, civilization in such instances easily becomes synonymous with a command of the language of the spiritual subjugators.

Uthman Dan Fodio's jihad, which constituted the major cultural event in 19th century northern Nigeria, was both a religious and intellectual movement. It accelerated and expanded the use of Arabic in literature, administration, and justice. By the end of the century, Islam and Arabic imperial structure had become the order of the day (Hisket 1975). Mecca had become the region's spiritual center while the validation of all intellectual ability among the powerful class was exclusively on the basis of its patrimony with Arabic. And, of course, when local languages came to be written eventually, the Arabic script formed the basis. As will become clear in the subsequent discussion of the spread of Christianity and English, the same pattern was replicated by the British conquest of the South.

The 20th century proved most critical for the development of Western education: it significantly transformed and altered Nigerian society. English was its principal means of delivery. There were three important dimensions to this implantation of English through Western education: the missionary enterprise, government policies, and the reaction of the local population.

C. 1. The Missionary Enterprise

Christian missionaries were indeed the principal vehicle of Western education in Nigeria between 1842 and 1882. In fact, after the establishment of the Colony of Lagos the missionaries continued to monopolize education for at least another twenty years. The three major Christian missions involved in this enterprise were the Wesleyan Mission, the Church Missionary Society, and the Roman Catholic Mission.

In Nigeria, as in other British colonies, education was the key, or the carrot, to Christian evangelism. The Wesleyan Mission led the way in the establishment of the foundations of Western education with the opening of the first school in Badagry by The Rev. Thomas Freeman and Mr. and Mrs. De Graft in 1842 (Hilliard 1957). Another school was subsequently opened in Abeokuta. Within the first forty years, the number of schools run by the mission had grown to include the following: two secondary schools (one for boys and the other for girls), one teacher training college, and nine elementary and primary schools.

English was a prominent subject in these schools. The boys secondary schools taught "ordinary English subjects" in addition to French, Latin, and Greek, while the girls school also taught "ordinary English subjects" in addition to French. It is important to note that the medium of instruction was English. The elementary schools used both English and the "vernacular"--Yoruba as media of instruction. They also taught English Reading, English Writing, as well as Yoruba Reading and. Yoruba Composition. Besides the fact that they taught Yoruba, what is perhaps most significant about the schools was the fact that the textbooks used in teaching were basically the same as those used in British primary schools, and were "expressly prepared to meet the requirements of the Educational Code of

England".

Although it began operating three years after the Wesleyan Mission, the Church Missionary Society (C. M. S) had become the dominant mission by 1882, its most easily remembered achievement being the establishment of the C. M. S. Grammar School at Broad Street in 1859. In addition to this, the mission established two teacher training institutions (one for men and another for women) as well as seventeen elementary and primary schools.

In the secondary schools, several activities involved the learning and use of English: Reading, Writing, Dictation, English Grammar and Analysis, English Composition and Recitation--six out of the fourteen subjects taught. It is also instructive to note that, between them, these English classes accounted for a total of 8 hours of the 31 school hours per week, that is, more than 25% of the school time. In addition, English was the medium used to teach all other school subjects. Latin and Greek were also compulsory subjects, besides, of course, English History, Roman History, and Greek History. Elementary school subjects included English Composition, English Grammar, Reading, Writing, and Dictation. English was the medium of instruction and, in infant schools, although Yoruba was the medium of instruction, Reading, Writing, Ciphering, and Dictation remained the major subjects.

Later, other missionary groups such as the American Baptist Convention and the Roman Catholic Church began to establish their own mission schools. By 1882, the Roman Catholic Mission ran five schools: one secondary school (St. Gregory's College), two elementary schools, and two infant schools. Until 1876, all education in the Roman Catholic mission schools was given in Portuguese because most of the native Catholic teachers were former slaves who had returned from Brazil.

The American Baptist Mission had the least number of schools--only one primary school in Lagos in 1882. The subjects taught included Reading Writing, Grammar, and Yoruba. Like their Wesleyan counterparts, the Baptists apparently prided themselves on using text books "taught in the Public Schools of [America]" (*Document Series CSO.1/2, CSO.1/10, CSO.1/11*).

The initial objective of the missionaries was to produce Nigerians who were marginally literate. The bible and manual work were emphasized to the exclusion of virtually all else because, in the words of Thomas Buxton, "It is the

Bible and the plough that must regenerate Africa" (1851: 451). This partially explains the overwhelming emphasis on primary, but not secondary education, the latter which was considered superfluous and likely to breed in the natives "materialism and intellectual arrogance".

It is also obvious from this brief review that right from the humble beginning of Western education through missionary effort and throughout the later history of education in Nigeria and elsewhere in Africa, the problem of language in education has constantly recurred. On the part of the missionaries, to the extent that they had any language policy at all it was pragmatic. For example, the principal medium of instruction in the Badagry and Abeokuta schools was Yoruba, the indigenous language of the area. But English was also used. The missionaries especially encouraged the development of literacy in the local languages so that the new converts could spread the gospel more easily to their illiterate kin. Literacy in the indigenous languages was thus considered the most effective means of proselytizing.

A comparison with the situation in other African countries offers similar and yet sometimes different examples. As reported in Laitin (1992), Congo Free State provides a very striking example of the interplay of language, power, and education in the colonial milieu. Somewhat similar to the practice of the missions in Nigeria, the Protestant missionaries used indigenous mother tongues for education in the villages. But as the competition for the soul of the African who, according to the catechist in Kenjo Jumbam's *The White Man of God*, had actually killed Jesus Christ, intensified, the Catholic missions moved next to the plantations, and began to use the regional lingua franca in the education of the children of conscripted workers (a.k.a. slaves) as well as freed slaves. A pragmatic reason for this development was the diverse linguistic backgrounds of the pupils (Laitin 1992).

The fact that none of the Protestant missions was Belgian and were therefore not subject to his influence caused King Leopold of Belgium considerable anguish. Yet, there was little he could do by way of direct interference in the missionary activities: the Berlin Act of 1884 by virtue of which he had been ceded the colony expressly prohibited him from denying the missionaries the right to proselytize. Not to be completely outwitted however in his desire to contain missionary influence, he promulgated the Education Act of

1890 which declared French the medium of missionary instruction. But he failed to achieve his objective because of the influence of the Parti Catholique which held power in Brussels. According to the Director of the justice and education departments, education in French would "induce students to avoid manual labor; they would become declasse, even anarchists" (Laitin 1992: 88). This conflict between the governing authority and the missions in Congo illustrates a significant theme: By standing behind the lingua francas of the Congo, the Catholics "were able to establish a protected market in conversions, even if those converts were of little use to the growing administrative apparatus, which had to look elsewhere ... for linguistically compatible servants" (Laitin 1992: 88).

I would like to mention briefly the Muslim missionary impact. In contrast to Christian missions, the Muslims were guided by functional domains. There was no doubt in their minds that Arabic was the appropriate medium in which to present the Hadith. Indeed, as Laitin correctly notes, "No matter where one travels in Muslim Africa, people have a general knowledge of the key suras in classical Arabic....[and] Often this is the limit of local knowledge of Arabic" (1992: 89). Of course, in North Africa Arabic was also a mother tongue and language of state. Although Arabic had not been actively cultivated for use outside the domain of religion, the Islamic rulers saw the threat of Western education offered in English. This had important consequences for education and politics in several African states, including Nigeria, as I will point out shortly.

C. 2. Language Policies of the Colonial Administration

The missionaries remained eclectic in their choice of the language of education for as long as they alone were directly involved in education. This state of affairs was however brought to an end in 1882 with the passing of Ordinance No. 4--the first Education Ordinance of the Gold Coast Colony (Between 1874 and 1884 the Settlement of Lagos was administered as an integral part of the Gold Coast Colony). The source of the information here is principally *Document Series CSO.1/1, CSO.1/10* and *CSO.1/11*--the Despatches of the Administrator of Lagos to and from the Governor of the Gold Coast. The Ordinance effectively declared English the language of instruction in all schools.

We must be clear as to the goals of the British in enhancing the position of English in the school system of their colonies. The primary interest of the British in promoting English was the desire to train a core of low level workers, clerks, typists, accounting clerks, interpreters, and telegraph operators to assist the colonial administration. In fact, while their education policy emphasized the learning of English on the one hand, the British simultaneously did try to discourage any widespread acquisition of English. They were distressed for one thing by the flood of petitions written in good English which the Colonial Office in London was getting. The military officers also feared that knowledge of English would provide Africans with access to sensitive information. It seems obvious, therefore, that the government's ambivalence parallels in some sense the ambivalence of the European missionaries too. Like the Christian missionaries, the British officials were persistent in discouraging Africans from "losing their identity", although, as we shall see presently, this attitude was held suspect by many Africans.

It is also worth noting that, in their goals, the British were not much different from other colonial powers in Africa. The Germans, as reported by Vander Ploeg, for example, practiced similar policies in their African colonies. School teachers who introduced the use of German in their schools in Cameroon were roundly castigated by the Germans (Ploeg 1977: 91-109).

The 1882 Education Ordinance (revised in 1887) altered the practice in the mission schools and accelerated the hegemony of English. The Phelps-Stokes Education Commission which visited Africa between 1919 and 1924 at the instance of the Baptist Mission in fact recommended that the language of the European nation in control should be used at the higher levels of primary education as well as taught as a school subject. Its recommendation that these languages also be the first to be taught in secondary schools agrees with the colonial government's goals in the reason it advances for the recommendations: "Native leadership must be able to confer freely with the government" (Jones, quoted in Omolewa 1985: 7).

With government intervention in education came the institutionalization of a certification system. This system further enhanced the position of English. In this regard, Omolewa makes the following observation:

> The certification system...ensured the ascendancy of English language, British studies, history, geography and politics as demonstrated by the curriculum and conditions of certificate

awards. (1975: 105)

At the Yaba College, for example, trainee science teachers had to take English as a subsidiary subject throughout their training, and there was even a proposal that, during their one year of practical training, they should take compulsory English classes.

Other government policy statements followed. But even though some of the controversies which surrounded a number of these policies are interesting and sometimes illuminating, they did little either in theory, or in practice, to change the status quo. For example, although it urged a study of the indigenous languages and the preparation of English texts more suitable to local conditions, the Advisory Committee on Native Education in Tropical Africa which was set up by the British Colonial Office in 1925 did not revise the existing arrangement for the teaching and learning of English in the colonies. In fact, it concluded by stressing the importance of acquiring English on three major grounds:

(1)   The educational value of English and the inadequacy of the native languages.

(2)   The need for English in the development of the territories.

(3)   The strong and natural demand of the natives for English. (Scott 1980: 26)

In the period 1882-1960, educational language policies and practices progressed more by imprecision than by clear direction. An internal memorandum on the use of "the Vernacular in education" by the then Acting Director of Education for the Northern Provinces most clearly spells out the prevalent colonial policy on language (English and indigenous). While stating that Nigerians had a right to be educated through their mother tongues as a means of "maintaining the good that there is in native customs," it specifically enunciates the following principles:

(b)   ...it is only through the vernaculars that the result of Western knowledge can be conveyed to the masses of the people;...

(c)   ...a knowledge of English by a certain number of the population is necessary for the acquisition of this Western knowledge, and for the economic development of Nigeria.

The knowledge of English must be thorough and reach a level at which it is possible to use and to enjoy the use of the language.

2. ...(1) The first aim of Government must be to give an elementary education to all the youth of the country, the vast majority of whom must remain in agricultural or pastoral pursuits if the country is to prosper. Discourage the use of the vernacular, and school pupils will be out of sympathy with their parents and whatever is good in native customs and modes of life will tend to disappear together with the desire to follow the parents' pursuits.

(2) The second aim must be to give a higher education -- and this it is generally agreed ...can only be given through a European language-- to a certain number of the youth, who will then become qualified to undertake the technical and clerical work at present mainly performed by aliens and in time no doubt to practise as Doctors, Engineers, etc., and who will be able to pass one some of the knowledge thus acquired to their parents and to the community at large... the following has been, and still, is the policy adopted with regard to the vernacular. In the Rural (Elementary) Schools, ...all instruction is given in the native language... In Provincial (Primary) Schools, to which few Rural Schools pupils will proceed, the vernacular continues to be the medium of instruction but in the Higher Forms English is included in the curriculum. (*CSO 26.16303*: 1-3)

A number of the linguistic and political goals of the British government are clear from the memorandum above. First, proficiency in English is to be reserved for a small intelligentsia. This implies the creation of a class-structured society with access to elite status, or the lack thereof, based primarily on the acquisition of English. English thus becomes a principal instrument of power. Second, the corollary, of course, is that the masses will be kept in their place by their retention of monolingual status. Third, English, like other European languages, is the appropriate, or suitable, medium for the primary apprehension of modern (Western) knowledge. Finally, there is a clear recognition of the fact that the apprehension of culture is primarily via language, and that to acquire a second language is to acquire a second culture. More importantly, in a colonial situation of unequal exchange, it is more probably to lose one--the First Language (L1) and first culture. There is, thus, a significant appreciation of the power and ideological dynamics of second language acquisition and use, with its potential for language and culture shift.

Other internal memoranda between various colonial education officers further reveal the difficulties and confusion of implementing the stated language policies. In addition, they often show great insight on the part of some expatriate officers into the significance of indigenous languages for the continuity of local cultural authenticity as illustrated in the memorandum above. One other such example, is the series of memoranda on the "Development of Mission Middle Schools" (*CSO 26.23889*). The following comments by T. H. Baldwin, Acting Assistant Director of Education, Northern Provinces in 1944, demonstrate both a keen sensitivity to the intolerable, schizophrenic linguistic situation of educated Nigerians as well as a realization of the practical dilemma which confronted educators:

> In an ideal world there is no conflict between the claims of the vernacular and a foreign language. On the contrary, a literary command of the one is an aid to acquiring the other while the foreign tongue, in turn fertilises the vernacular. Conversely, the superposition of a foreign language - especially if the latter is much more highly developed - on a weak vernacular foundation, leads to feebleness in both. This is seen on a large scale in the Southern Provinces. No one, I think, who has had to read through candidates' answers in the Elementary or Higher Elementary Certificate [Examination] can doubt it. Even where the English is tolerably correct it may be very difficult to discover what the man is thinking. **He is the victim of words, not their master.** [emphasis mine] (273c)

Writing in similar vein, R. A. McL. Davidson, National Director of Education, notes:

> ...It is in the mother tongue that everyone naturally thinks, can best form feelings and ideas for himself and can best express them to others. It is through his love and reverence for his mother tongue that an African can really be an African; and it is as an African that he properly takes his place as a member of the British Empire and a

citizen of the world. For its own sake, therefore, every African community should do all that is possible to preserve and foster its language. At the same time, however, it is reasonable to urge that English should be taught as a school subject in the elementary schools where the vernacular is the medium of instruction". (275)

Other colonial powers in Africa often pursued policies somewhat different from that of the British. But in each case these policies were dictated by what they considered to be in their own interest rather that of their African subjects. French language policy in Africa, for example, was significantly influenced by the fact that, at home, Third Republic France herself was still engaged in a process of language rationalization, a policy that was therefore extended to her African colonies. In parts of West Africa, French was considered a necessary counterforce to the advance of Arabic which the French--especially, given their experience in Algeria-- considered to be no more than a "proxy for Islam, fanaticism, and rebellion". By far the most often mentioned motivation for the French policy of promoting their language, however, is the French "moral quest" enunciated in their policy of assimilation.

The policy in the Portuguese-held colonies was initially decidedly anti-other European power, which meant anti-English and French. In 1903, the use of English was forbidden in Angolan schools, for example. But once the Portuguese had succeeded in arresting British and French influence, their policy became anti-African mother tongues. In pursuit of this new goal, Decree 77 of 1921 was promulgated. It expressly banned the use of African languages in all schools, and also prohibited any publication in these languages unless it is a parallel text to a Portuguese one. Finally, in 1950, Portuguese became the sole medium of instruction in all schools, public and private (Henderson 1979, Newitt 1987). In the Belgian Congo, the Belgian strategy was first and foremost to avoid multilingualism. If this prove impossible, then the languages in the national repertoire were to be ranked, with French naturally at the apex. In this event, African languages were to be helped to develop "rationally", a position which was to aid the regional vehicular languages (Laitin 1992).

The situation in Tanzania, which at various times was under German and British occupation, was strikingly different from that in virtually all other colonized African territories. With a population of about 15 million and just over 100 African languages, an African language, Swahili, was able to emerge as a dominant language in colonial policy. Whiteley (1969) has correctly noted the fact that there existed important social conditions which facilitated the evolution of Swahili in Tanzania. Among others, they include the response of the colonial administrations, educational institutions, and the missionaries to the country's linguistic diversity.

As early as the 18th century, Swahili was spoken all along the East African coast. Arab traders had spread the language and, in the process, facilitated the development of a common variant. In the latter half of the 19th century, European explorers and missionaries began to penetrate the Tanganyikan hinterland. By the 1880s, Arab influence had virtually evaporated, as they lost their often tenuous hold on the interior trade to the agents of German companies. When the Germans eventually took over the area then known as Tanganyika and declared it a protectorate to be administered by the German Foreign office in the last decade of the 19th century (O'Barr 1976), Swahili was not only well-established as a vehicular language, but was also appropriated as the language of colonial administration, a development virtually unparalleled elsewhere in colonial Africa.

When Britain assumed control of Tanganyika under a mandate from the League of Nations in 1920, the policy continued in some respects. In late 1920s, the Zanzibar dialect was selected over the Mombassa variety as the model for Standard Swahili, and in 1930, the Interterritorial Committee was established to standardize Swahili throughout British East Africa (O'Barr 1976). But the importance of Swahili in colonial administration was also seriously curtailed. For example, when the first legislative council was established by Sir Donald Cameron in 1926, English was the language in which it conducted business. It consisted of thirteen senior government officials and seven nominated members--five European, and two Asian. As Cameron is said to have noted, "no African could be found with a sufficient command of the English language to take part in the debates of the council" (Listowel 1968: 79 quoted in O'Barr 1976). By 1945, he apparently had found four African members who "could speak English". Between 1958 and 1960, elected members expanded the number of Africans in the body; but the Constitution still required members to be able to read and understand English (Tordoff 1967: 192). In this period of Tanzania's evolution, English therefore carried considerable prestige, not unlike in other British dominated African territories. European and Asian minorities found in English a symbol of their separateness from (and, no doubt, perceived superiority to) the Africans. Swahili was the language to use with inferiors such as household servants, office assistants, and the masses at large.

As Jean O'Barr has also noted, the rise of nationalism in then Tanganyika helped to reverse the potential decline of Swahili's prestige in the national speech repertoire and to promote its national status: "As people grew in political consciousness and became aware of the possibility of independence, Swahili became the mode for expressing that awareness" (1976: 70). In the forefront of this movement was the Tanganyika African Association which later metamorphosed into the Tanzanian African National Union (TANU). It not only wrote its constitution in Swahili, but also used Swahili as the language of political organization, in stark contrast to most other African nationalists whose only common vehicle was invariably the language of their colonial domination. As reported by Abdulaziz, when during the 1947 annual meeting of the Tanganyika African Association held in Zanzibar and which featured delegates from all over the country the Chairman chose English for his opening address, "a number of delegates protested and demanded that the speech be translated into Swahili... From that incident it was agreed that all future T.A.A. [Tanzanian African Association] meetings should be conducted wholly in Swahili" (1971: 165). As successor to T.A.A, TANU adopted the same position in 1954.

Several important developments in colonial education policies also facilitated the evolution of Swahili. During the period of German occupation, they had established three different types of schools. There were 60 Villages Schools ("Nebenschulen") which provided three years of schooling in Swahili. Next were 9 Middle Schools ("Hauptschulen") whose two-year course of instruction included Reading Writing, and Arithmetic. Finally, there was 1 High School ("Oberschule") whose menu featured clerical, industrial, and teacher-training education (Cameron & Dodd 1970: 56).

Under the British, Swahili continued to feature prominently in public schools. The Education Ordinance and Regulations which came into force in 1928 encouraged the use of Swahili and English in grant-aided schools (Eggert 1970). In the mid-1930s, Grade II teachers colleges (which provided a two-year training for potential elementary school teachers) were run in Swahili, while Grade I schools (which provided four years of education) used English. Obviously, then, there was a ranking which encouraged the acquisition of English and which also made its acquisition potentially more economically and socially rewarding. But this trend was somewhat countered by the familiar British snobbish attitude to those they had colonized, which was "to develop the people, as far as possible, on their own values and customs, purified where necessary" (Cameron & Dodd 1979: 14). In spite of this and the fact that, as the language of colonial administration, the use of Swahili was often a mark of "condescension and social distance", one cannot but agree with Abdulaziz's conclusion:

> By 1950... Tanganyika had emerged as a territory unique among all the multilingual territories of Africa, in having an African language widely spoken as a lingua franca and extensively used in the administrative and educational systems of the country. It was also remarkable that Swahili encountered little, if any, real competition or resentment from the over one hundred vernacular communities.
> (1980: 143)

By and large, Tanzanians were thus spared much of the psychological trauma that was to be the fate of many of their similarly colonized African brethren.

C. 3. The Response of the Local Population

In Nigeria, as in other African British colonies, several people strove tirelessly to acquire a mastery of English. This determination was predicated upon their appreciation of the status of English and the practical benefits of its acquisition. Given the fact that colonial education was firmly rooted in the socioeconomic and political activities of the colonial territories, the importance accorded to English was understandable. To the Nigerian, education held the promise of a better economic status. As Nnoli has correctly noted,

> ...to the colonized Nigerian, education was a very scarce commodity. Entrance to a good colonial employment particularly in the South required some level of colonial education. Employment in a good office provided at one and the same time relatively high income, high security, high social status, and a good opportunity to escape from what in the new colonial environment had become tiresome, tedious, and non-lucrative traditional agricultural work.
> (1979: 67)

First, this observation illustrates the fact that Nigerians were being forced to acquire a new *linguistic habitus* in the process of acquiring English. Second, given the power constellations in the colonial milieu, they had to learn new rules for operating the *linguistic market*. Many even felt the need to acquire a new *bodily hexis* (such as twisting their necks as they spoke English) considered appropriate to the newly-acquired English symbolic capital to boot. In a political economy where education was used, as has always been the case, as a means of acquiring the cultural capital necessary for certification for inclusion into the higher levels of the power structure, the principal medium of that rite was English. Hence the resistance of Nigerians, like most other Africans, to the use of indigenous languages as education media.

Beside the pragmatic considerations which made the British emphasize the use of English in schools they also had an active interest in promoting both their language and culture around the world. The principal instrument for achieving this goal was the British Council which was established in 1935. The Council's 1940 charter expressly entrusted it with the promotion of "a wider knowledge of our United Kingdom of Great Britain and Northern Ireland and the English language abroad". To achieve this goal, the Council encouraged innovations in methods of teaching English and made literature and dictionaries readily accessible in its libraries.

Such availability and accessibility of reading material was yet another factor which aided the growth of English. In contrast to the situation in regard to the English language, the only reading material available in Yoruba--at that time the best-developed of the indigenous languages--were a grammar, translations of the Bible, hymn books, and a few other books on proverbs, riddles, and local histories. Yet, there was tremendous pressure on the educated to sound literary and well-read; and the way to demonstrate erudition was to interlace one's speech or writing with regular quotations from Shakespeare, Milton, and other British writers, in addition to other formulaic phrases to be found in religious and literary sources.

As a direct result, the combination of the factors above with the missionary influence led to the creation of a budding elite class whom Ayandele calls "deluded hybrids":

[They] were...mentally, religiously and culturally part of the British empire. They had all...accepted...the Western version of

Christianity, had adopted European names in favour of African ones, donned European dress, and regarded with reverence "...the language that Shakespeare spoke" as the only one worth speaking. (Ayandele 1974: 19)

Perhaps on no other group was the pressure stronger that teachers. English was, and in many cases still remains, a most visible symbol of the teacher's "power". Part of the aura that surrounds many a teacher of English, or indeed any of the arts subjects, is that he or she speaks "such good English", "good" usually being synonymous with "bookish". Perhaps nothing better illustrates the symbolic power of English than the following words from a song which many elementary schoolchildren chanted as they marched to the beat of music from the school band after the morning assembly:

Òrè mi, mo gb'óyinbo kan,	My friend, I've just heard
Ta ló lè túmò o rè?	a (new) English (word),
Tísà wa ló lè túmò rè, --	Who can tell me the meaning?
Im-po-si-bi-li-ty...	(Only) our teacher can, --
	(The word is)"impossibility"...

The words aptly sum up the presumed ability of the teacher to perform tasks that seem impossible, based on his knowledge of English. In other words, the symbolic ability of the teacher to perform the impossible is measured by his acquisition of English linguistic capital. What is perhaps most significant about all this is the fact that it was the differential in power relations between Britain and Nigeria--a differential predicated upon the colonial milieu which made possible the execution of such imperialist policies to the detriment of the national languages and cultures.

Besides the foregoing, there is yet a more sinister and complex dimension to the power differential between the English language and culture on the one hand, and the indigenous languages and cultures on the other. This concerns the spiritual and mental slavery which is usually a consequence of the colonization or subjugation of one group by the other. To this, there were two sides, both of which operated simultaneously and were intricately interwoven: that of the colonizer and that of the colonized. It is important that we note the fact that, in this and other similar situations involving symbolic power, people do not simply grant power to a language just because of some perceived advantage it offers them in an economic or political market place. As Bourdieu (1991) has emphasized, the exercise of power through symbolic exchange always rest on a foundation of shared belief. In Nigeria and other colonized countries of Africa and Asia, the ideology of colonial capitalism assured this necessary conclusion.

The ideology of colonial capitalism takes Rudyard Kipling's concept of "the white man's burden" as axiomatic. The aim of colonial capitalism as expounded upon and practiced by the colonial powers was the justification of Western rule in its proclaimed aim of "modernizing and civilizing" the societies which had been subjugated by the Western powers. It was an ideology which blamed the victims of colonial exploitation rather than the exploiters, an ideology which considered exploitation a form of education. The white man was best suited to exploit the resources of the colonized lands, whose peoples were either totally "uncivilized" and would soon degenerate, or as the case may be, revert to the level of the beast if left to their own devices. Therefore, no effort--or cruelty--was to be spared to convince both the Europeans and the victims of their oppression of the justification of European imperial designs.

Africans were not the sole beneficiaries of this most remarkable tenet of European philosophical generosity. As Syed Hussein Alatas has correctly argued in his most illuminating consideration of the working of the ideology in Southeast Asia,

> Whether it was in Malaysia, the Philippines or Indonesia, or whether it was the British, the Spaniards or the Dutch, the same type of arguments prevailed. The historical forms of the civilizing process differed. Catholicism in Malaysia and Indonesia, for example, was not considered necessary to the civilizing process as it was in the Philippines. But all three powers agreed that Western rule and Western culture were superior; that Western peoples should lead the world; that they were most suited to exploit the natural wealth of the East; and that they were the best administrators. Consequently, the ideology of colonial capitalism played down the capacities of Southeast Asian societies. Every conceivable item was invoked to denigrate the Southeast Asian, including his size and physiognomy.(1977: 7)

The impact of this philosophy on Nigerians, as well as other Africans, was dramatic, especially given the manner in which they had been conquered. Many colonized peoples themselves bought into this ideology. The relationship between the colonizer and the colonized thus became symbiotic, much like that between the oppressed and the oppressor where, in Freireian terms, the oppressed internalize the consciousness of their oppressor. To become like the oppressor in fact becomes a subconscious goal.

The Igbo people of eastern Nigeria offer a clear illustration of how this situation unfolded. They had given stiff resistance to the British incursions, and so had had to be subjugated by force piecemeal. They had in fact erroneously assumed themselves and their gods to be more than a match for the British. But having been so unceremoniously routed time and again, these proud people were totally disillusioned. Not only had the traditional military machine failed them, even the time-honored gods and medicine men had deserted them. (Chinua Achebe's fictional accounts in *Things Fall Apart* and *Arrow of God* are particularly illuminating). Consequently, the Igbo not only bought into the ideology of colonial capitalism, but virtually went overboard. They were eager to acquire the white man's "magic". For them this became a quest, one which was readily reinforced by what Afigbo (1980) describes as "a traditional [Igbo] tendency to imbibe new ways as long as they worked". They were determined to transform the Igbo society along Western lines. The missionaries reinforced this state of mind by insisting to the Igbo that a necessary pre-condition for becoming good Christians or attaining salvation was the embrace of Western models in everything. And Western education given in English was the key to acculturation. The Igbo initially began by sending the slaves and "undesirables", who were observed progressing in the new dispensation. Thereafter, the initial trickle of pupils became an avalanche as the Igbo rushed en masse to the schools.

Mastery of English was indeed crucial to the acculturation process. It was like the magic key to the white man's knowledge, and they were not going to be cheated, as the following excerpt would suggest:

...when vernacular was introduced in the adult schools in Eastern Nigeria, students withdrew from classes. The Headmaster of Afikpo Government School in Ogoja Province reported in January 1945 that "the average native man sees no good in his being taught to read and write in his own vernacular". And when earlier on, in 1932, prospective teachers were encouraged by the Mission decisions to restrict education to the vernacular after their training, J. W. Welch, Principal of C.M.S. Oleh, explained that "This was a very unpopular move, for education to the native is too often comprised in the phrase 'knowing English'.". (Omolewa 1975: 109)

As in other parts of Africa, the missionaries were quick to exploit such developments to their proselytizing advantage. According to Nwoye (1978), while the Protestants continued to promote Igbo, the Catholics promoted English and became the dominant Christian faith, a position they have occupied ever since in that part of Nigeria. But it should be noted that the missionaries--apparently appreciating the maxim which Malcom X has now made famous (or infamous)-- were not averse to using "any means necessary," including using languages that did not carry the same prestige as did the European languages. What was important was the influence that they and their potential clients perceived a language to have in the market place. Thus, in Dar es Salaam, Tanzania, the Catholics used the lingua franca, Swahili. Seeing that they were fast losing ground to the Catholics, the Protestants reluctantly switched to Swahili too in hopes of picking up more converts (Barton 1980). In Gambia, a perceived threat from Muslim encroachment even led to a switch from English-medium education to Wolof (Laitin 1992).

Although the pattern of the pacification of Yorubaland to the southwest had been somewhat different from that of the Igbo in the East, their reaction to the colonial situation had not been much different. According to Asiwaju (1980), British penetration without the concomitant use of overwhelming firepower had been facilitated by the contemporary European diplomatic moves and the belligerent internal conditions of Yorubaland. First, the Anglo-French Agreement of August 10 1889 had defined the present-day Nigeria-Benin boundary south of latitude 9° N--leaving the British all parts of Yorubaland east of the line. Second, the Yoruba Wars of the mid-1800s and Dahomean forays into Egbaland led to British intervention as "peace-makers" and "protectors" respectively. In fact, British mediation in the Yoruba Wars, which by then had left the states considerably weakened both economically and militarily, ended with "protectorate" treaties in 1893. Meanwhile, the Benin Expedition also ended with the pacification of the Western Niger Delta.

At the end of the day, the Yoruba found themselves at the mercy of new masters. Like the Igbo, they were determined to thrive in the new political economy, and Western education which was acquired via English seemed the only means. According to Omolewa (1975), the Yoruba behaved like their fellow Igbo:

> The Yoruba people did not take advantage of the several opportunities offered by the Institute [the Institute for African Languages and Cultures]. This is because their objectives were not identical. For while the Institute rightly emphasized the relevance of the vernacular, declaring that in modern education a child should receive instruction both in and through his mother tongue, and that "the child should learn to love and respect the mental heritage of his own people, and the natural and necessary expression of this heritage is the language," the Nigerian looked for the means of obtaining the command of English in preparation for the advantages it brought. (109)

In an attempt to be as English as possible, several Nigerians from the South, especially the Igbo, abandoned the traditional selection of names and began to use and give English names to their children. Omolewa's observations on how the mental and material colonization of Nigerians has contributed to the development of English is once again illuminating:

> One can rightly draw attention to the susceptibility of Nigerians to foreign educational ideas and concepts dating from the period in the sixteenth century when the Oba of Benin requested the Portuguese to take control of his son's education. Dame Magery Perham draws attention to the fashion current among educated Nigerians to have their children trained in England and make them "speak English the whole day every Sunday". She also notes that Mr. Sam Pearce, another Nigerian "would show visitors his American electric organ."...the English language had become a status symbol by the second decade of the twentieth century.

For Sir Clifford reported that

> The much abused term "scholar" (which throughout West Africa is indiscriminately applied by the native to any person who can scribble a few words of English, no matter how faulty the spelling, atrocious the grammar, or obscure the meaning of the words so written), carries with it a certain

> prestige, which is a sure allurement to the innate vanity of
> the West African (1975: 113).

If we ignore the obvious racist overtone of Sir Clifford's glib comment about "the innate vanity of the West African," the message is clear. This was the absurd, but logical, culmination of the importance arrogated to the English language in the colonial political economy of Nigeria.

The reaction of other Africans with similar colonial experience was not very different. Sumner, for example, reports the following incident which took place soon after the founding of the Church Missionary (C.M.S.) school at Basia in northern Sierra Leone in 1808:

> A conflict arose out of the situation between instructions of the C.M.S. to the missionaries with respect to the use of the Susu language at school, and the wishes of the people. To conciliate the people, both white and black, and to gain their good opinion they taught the children in the English language.
>
> The great object which the parents of the children had in sending them to school was their acquirement of the English language. Therefore, according to their strict instruction, not a word of Susu was allowed to be spoken in school...The Susu children began to speak English in about six weeks, and soon after they were able to read and write in the same language...This pleased their parents exceedingly. (1964: 14)

In Cameroon as well, teachers protested against the teaching of Douala, a major indigenous language, in the Victoria schools.

Once again, this attitude was not limited to Nigeria, nor indeed other African colonies alone; it was prevalent in other places such as India that had suffered colonization. As Dakin reports:

> The learned natives of India were not slow to realize that a study of Western sciences, particularly when this led to preferential treatment in selection for government service as it did after Lord Hardinge's Proclamation of 1844, was more advantageous for their sons than the older Indian systems...When a Committee of Public Instruction was appointed to dispose of the annual grant in 1823, it found that all but one of the colleges and elementary schools in

existence were employing Arabic and Sanskrit. But already a new attitude was forming. When the Committee proposed to found a new Sanskrit seminary in Calcutta, Ram Mohan Roy wrote to Lord Amherst, the Governor General, protesting that 'the Sanskrit system of education would be calculated to keep this country in darkness.' Roy felt that there was an incompatibility between the medium of the old education and the content of the new. If the British wanted to encourage the spread of Western knowledge, they could not do it in the old language of religious learning. (1968: 5-6)

Although much credit has not been given to Nigerians in this respect, similar sentiments also contributed to their determination to master the English language thoroughly. There was more than a little suspicion of the British goals in education. Not a few Nigerians believed, and with good reason, that the British did not want them to be properly educated. And one way to achieve this goal would have been to deny them access to the one tool which would unlock the secrets of the books--English.

Before I begin to evaluate the consequences of the hegemony of English on the society and the emergent middle class, I would briefly like to consider the fate of English in the North. The pattern of British penetration of the North was similar to that of the East. The so-called Northern Provinces were conquered in stages between 1885 (in a series of campaigns started by the Royal Niger Company (RNC) and continuing under direct British government intervention after the RNC's charter was revoked in 1900) and 1903, following the defeat of Sultan Atahiru of the Sokoto Caliphate (Abubakar 1980). Given the similarity in the pattern of pacification of the North and the East, one might have expected the consequences to have been similar. However, for a number of reasons, this was not to be the case. First, the British met with a firmly entrenched religion and foreign civilization--Islam and Arabic culture. It was easier for the British to retain and exploit the already centralized administrative structures that they found. Also, given the sheer mass of the area, they lacked the personnel to directly administer the new territory.

In addition to these reasons, the British had already begun to regret the spread of education to southerners, first by the Christian missions, and later by the British government itself. The "ingrates" had become arrogant and were beginning to agitate against the British. Therefore, this time around the government took charge of education and restricted the Christian missions from evangelical, and therefore educational, activities. But little Western education was provided, and this only to the children of the ruling elite. Furthermore, given the feudal social and administrative arrangement in place, Western education was not a criterion for social mobility. What mattered was progeny and the favor of the rulers. This meant that, unlike the situation which obtained in the South, the key to Western education--the English language--was of little value.

Contrary to their public proclamations, the northern rulers also resisted any concessions to the English language, which to them was the symbol of the "decadent" Western education and culture and a potential source of the dilution of their absolute power over the masses. R. A. McL Davidson, once again, captures the true situation:

> ...when Emirs express a predilection for English to distinguished visitors they are saying what they think these visitors would wish them to say and not what they themselves feel. Alternatively they may wish that a few privileged servants of the Native Administrations may acquire a linguistic equipment which perchance may counter the penetrations from the South...the average school in the "deep North" is not "community centred"; it is usually "the District Head's School" and, as such, tends to be as moribund as the feudal system by which it is underpinned. Perhaps one way of dealing with this would be to withdraw Education Officers from the "deep North" and concentrate them in the pagan areas and the "Middle Belt". We might then touch the Emirs' prestige (which, I believe, is a matter to which they attribute importance) and thus bring about a situation whereby an educational system can be erected with some hope of success. (CSO 26.23889: 276)

Therefore, in contrast to the Southern situation, several factors--social, economic, and political--discouraged the spread of English in the North. This difference between the North and the South would continue to significantly affect the relationship between the two and the political fate of the country. Sa'ad Abubakar, a Northern historian, has claimed that in the period of the struggle for self-determination in the early fifties,

> the struggle [in the South] was a question of Nigerianizing, which
> at that time meant the Western educated taking over the political
> and economic control of Nigeria. They were not concerned with
> altering the whole society and creating something new for the
> betterment of all. (1980: 481)

By contrast, he argues, the North was preoccupied not with such "mundane"
matters like political party associations, but rather with loftier goals such as "self-
reappraisal and critical attitude towards existing institutions with a view to drastic
changes" (481).

But the historical evidence lends no support to this position, which is
nothing more than a myopic romanticization of the more base and basic motives of
the Northern elite. This is supported by the observations of Davidson, cited earlier,
as well as his further comments from the same memorandum excerpted below:

> ...I have suggested earlier, but without your [the Assistant Director
> of Education, Northern Provinces] customary delicacy, that the
> apathy [to Western education and English] derives from the slave
> mentality of the peasantry. Nothing can be done without the Emir's
> permission; and whether the Emirs in the "deep North" really
> believe in education for the masses, I take leave to doubt. Sooner
> or later, and probably sooner rather than later, Government will
> have to tell these feudalists that if they do not govern in the interest
> of the masses, they will have to quit, together with their court
> entourage. In short, it will have to be made plain to them that they
> represent an anachronism which cannot be tolerated much longer in
> this technological age. ...
>
> 14.   Your paragraph 7.   The social environment again
> obtrudes itself. If the "holy men" insist on Arabic being taught and
> thus overweight the syllabus, the considerations in the preceding
> paragraph apply.
>
> 15.   Your Paragraph 8.   By all means let us concentrate
> on those areas where conditions for the spread of English are
> favourable. But from what I have written earlier, I am inclined to
> think that in certain areas conditions are unfavourable for the

> spread of literacy in English or of literacy in any other language
> including Hausa. They can only be made favourable by drastic
> administrative action. (277)

The truth of the matter, then, is that the perceived self-interest of the Northern
oligarchy, which coincided with those of some political officers of the British
administration, led to the discouragement of Western education and the English
language. Unfortunately for the North--and for the entire country at large--this
conspiracy has boomeranged, with lingering potentially disastrous consequences
for the process of state construction and consolidation in Nigeria. This is a
conclusion which John Paden's (1968) analysis of the impact of the larger
controversial position of Hausa has had on Nigerian politics. Henry Bretton's
paraphrase of Paden's conclusion in his chapter titled "Political Science, Language,
and Politics" in O'Barr & O'Barr's volume is particularly apt. He states that, in
Nigeria,

> Hausa came to be identified as a symbol of political intent, or as a
> prime political issue, by detrimentally opposed groups, each seeing
> in [Hausa] substantially different qualities or values. The traditional
> rulers of the Northern Region saw in Hausa a means of preserving
> their own cultural and political position relative to other competing
> groups in the South in an ethno-linguistically pluralist country
> undergoing rapid and dramatic changes. On the other hand, the
> other language groups and cultures, principally Yoruba and Ibo,
> saw in Hausa the spearhead of a hostile pressure, a wedge driven
> into their midst by elements they deemed inferior largely because
> they identified the North with opposition to progress. (1976: 447)

I will return to the currency--and potency--of this issue later in Chapter Three, as I
discuss current language policies and practice in Nigeria.

Thus far, we see that Nigerians, and most formally educated Africans for
that matter, demonstrated Bourdieu's thesis that symbolic domination presupposes
on the part of the primary victims "a form of complicity which is neither passive
submission to external constraint nor a free adherence to values". In this colonial
context, the interaction of the *linguistic habitus* and the *linguistic market* was
based upon what he has described as:

> dispositions which are impalpably inculcated, through a long and

slow process of acquisition, by the sanctions of the linguistic
market, and which are therefore adjusted, without any cynical
calculation or consciously expressed constraint, to the chances of
material and symbolic profit which the laws of price formation
characteristic of a given market objectively offer to the holders of a
given linguistic capital. (1991: 51)

D. The Consequences of Educational Language Policies and Practices

As I have noted earlier, to understand the importance of English in the
emergent Nigerian society, we need to understand the impact of Western
education, the principal tool of which was the English language. As Osoba and
Fajana have noted,

The dissemination of Western literary education in Nigeria has had
an impact of a revolutionary character, out of all proportion to its
spread among the population, on the course of development of the
Nigerian society. (1980: 585)

Its effects on the Nigerian languages and cultures are those which are immediately
obvious.

As stated in the previous discussion, in theory the colonial administration
expressed great interest in the development of the indigenous languages. For
example, besides the statements of goals and principles already reported in the
memoranda of the Department of Education, other important evidence exists.
While the French established the Institut Fondamental D'Afrique Noire in Senegal
to work on African languages, the British founded the School of Oriental and
African Studies (SOAS) in London, among other things to promote African
studies, including those of African languages. However, these proclamations and
gestures notwithstanding, the practice in the schools, coupled with the local
reaction and the reality of the colonial political economy only weakened the
indigenous languages and cultures.

One clear example of the linguistic consequences was evident in the
schools in the Colony of Lagos. The emphasis on the teaching of English,
especially after the enactment of the 1882 Education Ordinance, had important
negative consequences for the indigenous languages. As English grew in
importance, the prestige of the indigenous languages declined dramatically.

Yoruba, for instance, suffered considerable neglect in the schools. Its teaching became poorly organized and was relegated to the background. T. A. Awoniyi adduces some evidence in support of this claim:

1. Monitors, that is, pupils from the upper classes, were assigned to teach the Yoruba alphabets on wall charts while the best teachers were assigned to the upper classes to improve the teaching of English;

2. The teaching of Yoruba reading remained in an unsatisfactory condition...(and [was]) largely conducted in a mechanical way; and

3. An Inspector of Education declared in 1891 "Let English be the language. If, of course, the vernacular can be used to explain English, I can only say 'Do so'." (1975: 12)

Many schools went as far as prohibiting pupils from speaking their mother tongues on school grounds. Yet, given the fact that there is a real limit to the amount of information, especially at a cultural level, that can be translated into a second language (even if students had the requisite level of bilingual sophistication which, of course, they lacked), and also given other supportive factors, the accumulation of a predominantly English cultural capital was a foregone conclusion. The colonial goal of inculcating into students British middle class values was indeed being achieved. It was this kind of anomalous situation, especially in the first half of this century, that prompted the following observation by the Phelps Stokes Commission:

Native tongue is immensely more vital in that it is one of the chief means of preserving whatever is good in Native customs, ideas, and ideals...All peoples have an inherent right to their own personality however primitive they may be...No greater injustice can be committed against a people than to deprive them of their own language. (Omolewa 1975: 107)

Stripped of its condescending and somewhat disparaging undertone, this comment by the Phelps Stokes Commission still shows greater insight into the implications of the prevalent educational policies and practices than the colonial administration. It also echoed the thinking of some principal expatriate education officers as earlier documented.

One other feature of the school situation was a tendency to create a dichotomous relationship between traditional values and mores of the people and those of the school champions. Segun Osoba rightly observes a general "inverse ratio between the level of academic attainment and knowledge of such things as family and lineage traditions, folk music, dances and genres, which is automatically acquired in a purely indigenous milieu" (1980: 586). This alienation is reflected in another comment by the Phelps Stokes Commission:

> If the pupils were asked to sing any song they pleased, the chances were strong that we would hear "The British Grenadiers"!...When they are asked to sing an African song, a boat song, or any chant used in their own plays, a laugh invariably went through the whole class...Similarly, if we asked about history, we soon discovered what happened in 1066, but of their own story --nothing. (Nduka 1964: 39)

The colonization of Africa not only effected the linguistic balkanization of the continent, it also installed the metropolitan languages as the "proper" media of cognitive and inter-personal communication. Most Europeans would not learn the local languages. Therefore, for the Africans to exist meaningfully in the new world thus created by the Europeans, European languages such as English became the media for naming objects, expressing feelings, and executing other major speech acts. In consequence, therefore, "the acquisition and mastery of the languages of the colonizing powers...created a form of social stratification based on one's ability to communicate in French or English" (Jinadu 1976: 612).

The Christian missionaries also encouraged this trend. They encouraged converts, who formed the elite class, to become individualistic--set apart from the "extended" family and recognizing only their wife and children, and to look down upon his language. According to Ayandele, "As late as the closing decades of the nineteenth century, anglicized Africans and evangelists lamented that converts were not seen eating, or having a walk, with their wives" (1980: 360).

But the Europeans also despised the mimicry. They seemed to be saying to those who had learnt their lessons well indeed, "No, we won't have you pretending to be like us!". Educated converts became the laughing stock of all classes of Europeans, including the missionaries. They were torn between two cognitive and cultural worlds and bereft of permanent and solid roots in either. The serious problems of authenticity which arise concern not only the individuals, but also make cultural survival for the various indigenous communities more difficult. This is indeed the genesis of the schizophrenic existence of the Westernized elite class in Nigeria, and several other African countries today.

There were other linguistic and political consequences of the colonial language policies and practices. One was the creation of "linguistic minorities" as a result of the quest of some colonial education officers--and, later, ethnically-oriented politicians--for regional lingua franca. An example was the series of attempts to institutionalize Hausa as the lingua franca in the Northern Provinces, a policy which had already been questioned by R. A. McL. Davidson with characteristic bluntness and would later, along with other factors, cause serious political problems in the country:

> ...If Dr. East [Senior Education Officer i/c Literature Bureau] had said that Hausa was the mother tongue of a considerable portion of the North and should be cherished on that account, I should have agreed with him wholeheartedly. But I am disposed to think that the indiscriminate encouragement of Hausa as a lingua franca for large agglomerations of non-Hausa speaking peoples is wrong in principle and that, if such a process is encouraged for reasons of administrative convenience, or for any other reason, it will break down sooner or later. (*CSO 26.23889*: 276)

Speakers of the southern Nigerian languages also suffered in relation to Arabic and Hausa speakers in the North. This was principally as a result of the justice system. One of the judicial consequences of the 1914 Amalgamation of the Northern and Southern Protectorates was the merging of the previous two judicial systems. First, the two supreme courts were merged into one under a single Chief Justice and with one Attorney-General. Second, the Provincial Court system of the North was imported into the South. Below this were the "native" courts.

One major source of linguistic inequality was the Provincial Courts which were presided over by British political officers. Besides the facts that the presiding officers were not necessarily legally trained and that the courts were not open to African or expatriate lawyers, they were not immune from corruption. A principal source of corruption was language. Since the business was conducted in English, the court interpreter occupied a crucial role in the deliberations. And since more often than not those charged to the court would not be able to speak English, they were often at the mercy of the interpreter's incompetence or mischief.

The second linguistic inequality was localized to the North. The *Sabongaris* where most non-natives (southerners) lived had mixed courts, where attempts were made to accommodate the linguistic and cultural differences between the indigenous population and the southerners. For example, in Zaria and Kano between 1932 and 1954, the Presidents of the courts were Ghanaians and Sierra Leoneans, while the three Assessors were Hausa, Igbo and Yoruba. The customary laws of the litigants were enforced. But the "Native Courts" practiced Islamic Law of the Malikite School. Foreigners who lived outside distinct *Sabongaris* suffered both culturally and linguistically in these courts. In fact, between 1958 and 1959, the "native courts" were renamed Provincial Courts in the North and were presided over by Alkalis in the Muslim provinces.

There is perhaps one positive dimension to the spread of English in colonial Nigeria. But then, this is a double-edged sword. It has to do with the political sphere of the national life and the continent itself. English was the language of inter-ethnic communication among the nationalists who fought for Nigeria's independence. As Ali Mazrui (1974) has rightly argued, although it was an alien language, for the nationalists English came to be regarded as the appropriate medium in which to express nationalistic aspirations. It helped them in two ways: first, it ensured the process of their political education, and second, it provided a common language for nationalists both within and outside the common boundaries of any given British colony.

The English language contributed significantly to the growth of Pan-Negroism. It was the language of the African Americans and several other Blacks in the Diaspora. It facilitated the contact between educated Africans and their kinsfolk in the New World. This contact is in fact largely responsible for the strong part which the English-speaking countries played in the Pan-African Movement, almost to the total exclusion of their French-speaking counterparts. Many African nationalists such as Nnamdi Azikiwe and Kwame Nkrumah had the opportunity to study not only in the homeland of their country's colonial master (Britain), but also in America where at least the rhetoric, if not the actual practice, of freedom was strong. They experienced racial discrimination and the Black struggles for equality in America, and this further fired their nationalistic feelings. All this was made possible through the use of the English language.

While some may advance the argument that, prior to such developments, there existed pockets of resistance to foreign domination, for example, among the Asante of Ghana, the resistance to foreign rule in English-speaking Africa did not really become nationalistic until its leaders became English speakers. Furthermore, the role of English in the independence struggle must be seen in the light of the different philosophies adopted by the British as opposed to the French in Africa. The French pursued their principle of "assimilation" and bred the likes of Leopold Sedar Senghor. The British, in contrast, sought no such goals. In French-speaking Africa, with the possible exception of Guinea, the consequence was "linguistic cosmopolitanism," with people like Senghor extolling the virtues of the French language over and above all others:

> If we had a choice we would have chosen French...First, it is a language which has enjoyed a far reaching influence and which still enjoys it in great measure. In the eighteenth century French was proposed and accepted as the universal language of culture. I know that today it comes after English, Chinese, and Russian in the number of people who speak it, and it is a language of fewer countries than English. But if quantity is lacking, there is quality...
>
> I am not claiming that French is superior to these other languages, either in beauty or in richness, but I do say that **it is the supreme language of communication**: "a language of politeness and honesty; a language of beauty and clarity"...[emphasis mine] (Senghor 1963: 10)

In English-speaking African countries such as Nigeria nationalism was the consequence of the colonial policies. It is however unfortunate that this nationalism did not really spread to matters of language choice and use. In fact, nationalist leaders like Nnamdi Azikiwe and Kingsley Mbadiwe specialized in demonstrating their ability to interlace their speech with lengthy--and often nonsensical--English words--which, invariably, impressed their less discerning audiences.

Thus, we see an unholy convergence of political, administrative, economic, and linguistic policies in the shaping of the course of history in much of Africa. I have already highlighted some of the major consequences of the importance of English in colonial Nigeria. One of these was the effective colonization of the mentality of the emergent society through acculturation to the English language and way of life. Here, the essential point remains that the use of an imported or colonial language in some form or the other promotes in the colonized the values and ideology of the exporting country or metropolis. Such acculturation is indeed not unfamiliar in other parts of the "Third World" subjected to colonialism.

Indigenous African languages which were derogatorily called "vernaculars" were also downgraded. If we recognize the intimate relationship between language and culture, then the downgrading of one cannot but be accompanied by that of the other. In the development of the consciousness of the first generation of educated Nigerians and other Africans, the internalization of English progressed with the internalization of the colonizer's world view. Education, indeed, also came to be confused with mastery of the English language.

Unfortunately, since Nigeria and most other African countries attained independence in the 60s, little has been done to change the role of English and other languages of colonial domination, or to arrest the devaluation of most indigenous African languages and cultures. The new challenges of state construction and consolidation and the harsh facts of Africa's post-independence economic realities, coupled with the cynical quest of most post-independence leaders for political legitimacy have only compounded the problems. Perhaps the only notable exceptions are Tanzania and Somalia whose own peculiar sociolinguistic configurations stand out in stark contrast to those of their sister nations. I will discuss Tanzania's case, in particular, in the next chapter.

CHAPTER THREE

LANGUAGE, STATE CONSTRUCTION , AND GROUP CONFLICT IN THE POST-INDEPENDENCE ERA

A. Introduction

Language policy decisions, both educational and political, constitute a recurrent backdrop against which the political sociology of language choice and use has to be analyzed. Therefore, it becomes necessary to preface a review of the post independence linguistic scenario in Africa with a consideration of the relevant language policy documents and instruments.

As has generally been the case in post-colonial African states, the rationale, or impetus for language policy decisions in Nigeria between independence in 1960 and the eve of the Third Republic in 1993 can be explained as a protracted attempt to come to terms with the competing and often politically conflicting problems of nationism and nationalism. As enunciated by Joshua Fishman (1968a, 1968b), nationalism grows out of the feeling of members of a sociocultural unit--a nationality--that they are united and identified with others who share a common history, culture, religion, and language. Nationism, on the other hand, is the driving force behind the more practical problems of constructing, consolidating, and governing what is a geo-political, but not necessarily a sociocultural, entity.

The conflict between the forces of nationism and nationalism is historical. And all too often it is complicated by the personal political interests of those who champion these two differing principles:

State leadership going back at least as far as the Roman Empire has sought to classify peoples and languages through the creation of boundaries where one language ends and another begins. Meanwhile, ambitious politicians have alternately sought to reify these boundaries and to undermine them for purposes of gaining power and wealth. (Laitin 1992: 7)

Language features prominently in the scenario because, even before independence, it had been accepted as being central to national unity. For example, a colonial governor in Nigeria, Sir Arthur Richards, had identified language as one of the major obstacles in achieving national unity in his 1945 proposals for the development of a Nigerian constitution. Other Nigerian politicians, notably the late Obafemi Awolowo, have also called for the creation of states whose geographic boundaries are coterminous with linguistic ones (Akinnaso 1987). In the thirty-year period immediately following independence, the government has sought to address this issue via educational, political (constitutional) and cultural policy instruments.

Before we can discuss the role of language in state construction, we need to ask ourselves, how do we describe the post-colonial state in Africa? Are modern African states "nations of many nations", that is, multinationality nations, or are they "nations of many tribes"? According to Laitin (1992) it is indeed fashionable even within the continent of Africa to call African countries nations of many "tribes". Herein lies a primary problem in the definition of language policies for Africa. If African nations consisted of just tribes, then it should be easy to rationalize language use, and probably just apply at least some weak form of the territoriality principle--which "seeks a degree of cultural and economic self-regulation, recognizing the hegemony of the center in nationwide and international concerns" (Fishman 1986: 117)--where necessary. However, the historical circumstances of the evolution of the nation-nation in Africa is of course not conducive to such a practice. Statehood was imposed on virtually all African countries, not by an indigenous power that could have maintained the spread and consolidation of a new linguistic culture in the process of its centralization of authority, but by an external power that could not stay around long enough to do so. If, for example, the power of the Hausa-Fulani oligarchy had not been supplanted by the British in 19th century Nigeria, such a situation could easily have developed not only in the northern parts of Nigeria, but also in the Middle-Belt, and perhaps even as far south as the northern Yoruba plains. After all, the jihad came as far south as Osogbo in Yorubaland.

The reality of Nigeria, like several other African countries, then, is that several societies at different stages of political development were arbitrarily brought together as one nation. Some, like the Oyo Empire, Benin Empire, and the Hausa-Fulani Empire had political cultures that in many respects were far advanced beyond what obtained in some European countries at the time of colonization. And each was defined by the existence of a common language, a result of the fact that the nation had evolved from a sociocultural entity (for example, Yoruba in the Oyo Empire, and Edo in the Benin Empire), or as a consequence of an ongoing *de facto* language rationalization (as was the case in the Hausa-Fulani Empire and the regions of the Middle-Belt under its occupation or influence). Often, outsiders, and occasionally some Africans too, wonder why African countries cannot simply each have one language. They often easily point to the example of Tanzania. It is of course easy for Julius Nyerere and others to advocate the cause of Swahili as Tanzania's national language--and even at times, Africa's. History lent them considerable support. But for virtually the rest of the continent, at least sub-Saharan Africa, the situation is not so easily resolved.

Laitin (1992) addresses these problems of language in nation building at some length. The easiest options for state construction in African multinationality nations come at such a high price:

> Nation building for Nigeria, Senegal, Ivory Coast, Ghana, and Zaire
> meant defining the nation--at least in its language component in
> foreign terms. How could the cultivation of English in Nigeria, or
> of French in Senegal, be called "nation" building? (Laitin 1992: 9)

With this observation in mind, Laitin tries to determine "how one component of the nation--language--gets pulled into the battle for the institutionalized domination over society by a ruling cadre, otherwise known as state building" (1992: 9). Important as Laitin's observations which I will discuss shortly are, he still misses a great deal of the complexity of the language situation in Africa. Is there only a ruling cadre in any country? Any ruling class is but one locus in the conflict of power and ideology, with language as proxy. The picture certainly seems much more complex: not only are there several competing groups, but there are competing individuals, nations, and ideologies. And language has been appropriated into each of these conflicts in Africa in a manner that is perhaps unparalleled anywhere else today. Laitin's limitation, I would like to note, are however imposed by the sensible constraints he has imposed upon his own study as the questions he set out to answer reveal.

B. Political Language Policy

The position in which African political and intellectual elites find themselves is by no means simple. They must defend the cultural integrity of their countries while at the same time moving forward rapidly with the business of state construction and economic development. Laitin captures their dilemma when he writes:

> At times [the elite] speak as champions of their own mother tongue,
> arguing that each of the languages of Africa reveals and preserves
> Africa's rich cultural heritage. Yet at other times these same
> intellectuals, or their ideological kin, passionately advocate a
> politics in which each country chooses a single, indigenous
> language as the official language of state. (1992: 4)

This but of course only presents an incomplete picture. At other times, the nationalism of the elite is only skin deep, functioning as nothing more than a veil for their quest for group or ethnic hegemony, an attempt at establishing "new equilibria" favorable to their own groups.

With the aid of game theory, Laitin (1992) analyzes the language situation in Africa and speculates on what are likely to be the dominant language policy models in African states. His study helps us to partially understand the complexity and historicity of Africa's sociolinguistic quagmires. In terms of possible language outcomes in Africa, Laitin contends that there are three possible scenarios: language rationalization, a "3±1" outcome, and a 2-language outcome.

Language rationalization has been the dominant European tradition. For example, such was the goal of King Francis when in 1539 he promulgated the Edict of Villers-Cotterets, investing the Ile-de-France dialect, Francien, with the prestige of official language of the empire. His goal was to counteract the influence of Latin, a goal which the expulsion of the Jesuits in 1762 finally ensured. But the process of successful rationalization in France took more than 300 years. This pattern has been replicated with local modifications in different regions. For example, Philip V of Spain enacted the Decree of the Nueva Planta in 1716 making Castilian the state language, while in Japan the Meiji period (1868-1912) witnessed the rationalization of Japanese dialects. Laitin believes that such a language outcome in which only one official or national language will be needed for social and economic mobility is likely only in Somalia, Tanzania, Botswana, Swaziland, Lesotho, Rwanda, Burundi, and Malagasy.

The 2-language outcome involves a mother tongue ("vernacular") and a "common international language". He projects this as the likely outcome in countries like Mozambique, Angola, Namibia, the Republic of South Africa, Togo, Morocco, Tunisia, and Zimbabwe. This of course leaves the majority of African countries in the third category: those with a "3$\pm$1" language outcome, which Laitin believes will be the norm, a situation which will be facilitated by the demands of "occupational mobility" and "middle-class urban opportunities". This scenario involves a primary language, which may or may not be the language in which an individual receives elementary education, an "African lingua franca" which will be promoted by "nationalist politicians" for extra-local communication, and a colonial language. Someone whose mother tongue is also the language of the "immediate community" (LIC) used for elementary education need only learn two more languages. Those whose mother tongue is not the language of the immediate community would however have to learn three additional languages. Those individuals whose mother tongues coincide with the LIC--and perhaps even the national "lingua franca"--may presumably get away with learning only one additional language, the erstwhile language of colonial domination. This, Laitin projects, is the likely outcome in countries like Nigeria, Zaire, Kenya, and Ethiopia. While Nigeria may seem to fit into Laitin's third category in several respects, there are also significant differences and complications introduced by the complexity of the interplay of language, power, and ideology with makes his assertion that Nigeria has "gone a long way toward a 3$\pm$1 outcome" highly suspect.

Ever since the dawn of independence in 1960, Nigeria like many other new nations in Africa has remained a country in transition. But it is often unclear into what it is being transformed. Shiva Naipaul (1979) attempts to capture this trauma of societal transition when he writes, perhaps excessively, that:

Transitional states are full of pain, riddled with illusion. We can

> lose one self without gaining another. Our development can be
> indefinitely arrested at the stage of caricature. (54)

This transitional stage gives rise to a number of conflicts generated by tensions between old and new values seeking preservation and affirmation respectively. Such conflicts and tensions are further accentuated in Nigeria by the country's cultural, religious and linguistic plurality, since the new countries of Africa were no more than convenient colonial creations. People of disparate tongues and cultures at different stages of sociocultural and political integration were arbitrarily grouped together. And, indeed, the reality of state building after independence has often forced some occasionally bizarre reversals in the stance of those previously fire-breathing nationalists of the independence struggle.

By the time Togo's Sylvanus Olympio was overthrown in a 1963 coup, he had instituted both Ewe and Hausa as co-official languages with French, the language of Togo's colonial domination. After the coup, however, French became the sole official language because, as the coup makers claimed (no doubt with French concurrence), "the old policies... stirred up ethnic tensions" (Kozelka 1984). In pre-1984 Guinea, the fiery nationalist Sekou Toure had vigorously promoted the indigenous languages. But the Comite Militaire de Redressment National which seized power that year reinstated French as the sole medium of education, claiming like their Togolese counterparts that previous language policies which favored indigenous languages were responsible for perceived economic and educational failures (Treffgarne 1986).

But in other countries the quest for the maintenance of power forced an appreciation of the symbolism of language. As Laitin (1992) reports, Cameroon's Ahidjo sought to promote indigenous languages when he felt his grip on power was threatened in 1976. Even more bizarre is the case of Zaire's Mobutu. In the 1960s, he had boasted to the world that his country "represented the second French-speaking country in the world" (Champion 1969: 1). But in the seventies, he suddenly rediscovered his Africanness: he not only changed his country's name from Congo Kinshasa to Zaire, but he also changed his own name from Joseph Mobutu to Mobutu Sese Seko. For good measure, he also subsequently banned the wearing of neckties, and promoted African hairstyles in women. The real motive of course had little to do with nationalism but had everything to do with establishing and consolidating the legitimacy of his power.

Some of the pressures for these changes in the position of African leaders on language policy also came from outside vested interests. For example, as Laitin (1992) notes, the rise of oil-power in the 1970s gave some oil-producing Middle Eastern countries considerable influence on the language policies of some African countries. They were in a position to give financial aid to poor African countries; but this aid came with strings. These African countries were required to promote Arabic education. For example, Somalia, which was the benefiary of substantial aid not only became a member of the Arab League, but also pursued Arabic education in its public schools. Arabic also attained co-official status with Somali. In Chad, Hissen Habre made Arabic a second official language in the process of enlisting Saudi Arabia's support in his conflict with Libya to the north. Finally, Mauritania made similar investment in Arabic in return for financial aid from Arab countries.

In the specific case of Nigeria, even though the final "pacification" may have come in 1914, for all practical purposes the country was administered as two separate entities: the predominantly Muslim north, and the largely Christian and traditional south. The political, cultural, religious, and educational disparities between these two groups delayed the independence of Nigeria by at least a few years and poisoned the political atmosphere in the immediate pre-independence period. The kind of tensions, and mutual suspicions that pervaded the atmosphere are expressed in these words from the autobiography of the Sardauna of Sokoto, leader of the ruling party in the First Republic and Premier of the Northern Region:

> As things were at the time [the early 1950s] if the gates to the [government] departments were to be opened, the Southern regions had a huge pool from which they could find suitable people, while we had hardly anyone. In the resulting scramble it would, we were convinced, be inevitable that the Southern applicants would get almost all the posts available. Once you get a government's post [sic] you are hard indeed to shift--[This] was a matter of life and death to us-- if the British administration had failed to give us the even development that we deserved and for which we craved so much-- and they were on the whole a very fair administration-- what had we to hope from an African administration, probably in the hands of a hostile party. The answer to our minds was, quite simply, just nothing, beyond a little window dressing. (Quoted in

Abernethy 1969: 413)

It is evident from the foregoing, then, that one of the problems the new nation would have to contend with would be the maintenance of the fragile unity which the British had imposed. Evidently, the English language as a non-indigenous common tongue--at least among the educated elite--provided a basis for the continuation and possible consolidation of this fragile unity. When after independence there was a call in the Federal Parliament for the adoption of an indigenous language, it was greeted with the following reaction by a Lagos-based newspaper, *The Daily Express:*

> Parliament should be more careful about involving itself in the language tangle into which it is now being drawn. English is the accepted official language, the one outward expression of all that unites the various peoples in this country...to seek to replace English with some vernacular at a particular dateline is asking for more than the greatest nationalist of them all can handle. (Brosnahan 1965: 24)

The post-colonial nation has continued to prove a veritable field for the quest for symbolic power. This quest for symbolic power normally works unobtrusively; it is carefully concealed under such slogans as "national dignity," "freedom," "independence," "national pride," and "national unity," to mention but a few. As defined by Bourdieu (1991), symbolic power is an invisible, and intangible, yet compellingly effective force which is exercised only with the tacit approval of those who do not want to know that they are victims of it, or that they exercise it. Blakar makes a similar point when he notes that "the language user's social influence is ... defined through effect or consequence, completely disregarding whether the effect is intended or not" (1979: 134).

Many of those whom Laitin calls "nationalists" would easily fit into this category of linguistic "carpet baggers". The various nationalities in Nigeria and other African countries are engaged in what constitutes a symbolic struggle whose goal is the imposition of a definition of the socioeconomic and political world that is best suited to their interests, that is, favourable "equilibria" (Laitin 1992). Normally, these struggles are pursued directly in the symbolic conflicts of daily life --the use of particular varieties, or languages, in various domains of national life-- home, school, work, etc., or by proxy. The latter describes the conflicts between different specialists in symbolic production, attempts to monopolize "legitimate symbolic violence", that is, the power to impose, or inculcate, "the arbitrary instruments of knowledge and expression (taxonomies) of social reality" whose truly arbitrary nature is not customarily recognized.

The conflicts are further complicated by the number of players and the nature of the tool--language. There are not only many contending forces, both national and international, but the means of symbolic power number in the hundreds in countries like Nigeria. The contending forces in Nigeria include, at one level, the Westernized elite class who have mastered the English language and presume themselves rich in the requisite Western cultural capital, and whose interests largely coincide with those of Western political powers. The civil servants in several African countries and India whose language preferences Laitin (1992) exhaustively discusses easily fit into this category. There are also the different ethnic groups which represent the former nations in the modern state, and the non-Westernized majority of the population. While the ultimate goal, power, remains constant, the symbolic means of the struggle changes depending on which cap the combatants sport at a particular point in time.

Suffice it to say at this point that the elite class has been the driving force behind all the various language policies, including the demand for indigenous "official" or "national" languages. Naturally, at no time has anyone ever asked ordinary Africans whether this constitutes an important issue to them or not. That is as it should be. After all, the goal is not to widen membership of the class in which power resides, but to further narrow it. In effect, therefore, the debates over language policy in state construction, as I will explain in some detail shortly, have really been only part of the struggle for power among contending groups in the nation-states, groups that wish to appropriate and monopolize the power that the erstwhile colonial masters once held.

Language as a central factor in this struggle for hegemony has added to the complexity of the struggles for power. The linguistic situation is indeed quite complex, involving as it does three major language types. There are the indigenous languages, estimated at about 400 (Hansford, Bendor-Samuel and Stanford 1976) for a population which, according to a 1987 Unesco estimate is today in the region of 110 million. These languages represent various language families and groups or subgroups of families: Afro-Asiatic (Hausa, Bachama), Nilo-Saharan (Kanuri,

Dendje) and Congo-Kordofanian (West Atlantic (Fulani), Mande (Busa), Voltaic (Bariba), Kwa (Igbo, Yoruba, Nupe), Benue-Congo (Tiv, Efik) and Adamawa-Eastern (Kam, Liba)) (Oyelaran 1991). In the second group are the "exogenous languages": English, French and Arabic (Akinnaso 1989). Finally, there is Pidgin, a "neo-language" (Oyelaran 1991).

The military intervention in national politics beginning with the first military *coup de tat* in 1966 established the practice of making language policy a constitutional matter in post-independence Nigeria. Consequently, the language question featured prominently in both the 1979 and the 1989 Constitutions. While the 1954 Constitution had declared English Nigeria's official language, there had been no move towards language rationalization in English. Laitin argues that "Nigeria because of its federal structure is furthest [of all African countries] along the line in consolidating a 3±1 framework" (1992: 21). He identifies three principal pressures for this type of language outcome. First, politicians appreciate the fact that an indigenous language would have considerable emotional appeal. Second, the federal structure encourages rationalization at the state level. Finally, the requirement for "federal character" in employment at the federal level and the continuing demands for new states also encourage this trend. But I believe that not only is Laitin's analysis of both the sources of the pressures incomplete, but his belief that Nigeria has progressed far on the path of a 3±1 outcome is only supported in principle.

Let us now look at the specific policy documents. The *Constitution of the Federal Republic of Nigeria 1979* provided for the use of three major Nigerian languages, in addition to English, in the Federal Senate and House of Representatives:

> 51. The business of the National Assembly shall be conducted in English and in Hausa, Ibo, and Yoruba when adequate arrangements have been made therefor.

At the state level, there are provisions to allow state legislatures to use one or more local languages, in addition to English, for legislative business:

> 91. The business of a House of Assembly shall be conducted in English, but the House may in addition to English conduct the business of the House in one or more other languages spoken in the State as the House may by resolution approve.

It is interesting to note the contrast between this and neighboring Ghana's 1969 Second Republic Constitution which requires that a federal legislator must be "able to speak and, *unless incapacitated by blindness or other physical cause*, to read the English language with a degree of proficiency sufficient to enable him to take an active part in the proceedings of the Assembly" (Article 7/[d]) [Emphasis mine]. Subsequently, there has been considerable pressure to substitute Akan (variously estimated as a first language for 42% of the population, and as a second language for 20%) for English (Laitin 1992: 131).

The second constitution to be hammered out by the military is *The Federal Republic of Nigeria Constitution, 1989*. Promulgated by decree in May 1989 and supposed to have come into effect in 1992 when the Third Republic was originally scheduled to take off, it will now presumably become effective on August 27, 1993. It has even more specific references to language. In respect of the fundamental objectives of the state, the Constitution declares the government's intention to promote the learning of indigenous languages (Section 19 (4)). Section 21 also declares that "The State shall protect, preserve and promote the Nigerian cultures ...". We may assume that this further implies the promotion of the indigenous languages as vehicles of culture.

In the legislatures, besides affirming the earlier provisions in the 1979 constitution, the 1989 constitution introduces new linguistic criteria. It has this to say in respect of the national legislature:

63. *Qualifications for election*:...(2) A person shall be qualified for election under subsection (1) of this section only if he has been educated up to at least the School Certificate level or its equivalent.

For the state legislatures, the requirements are the same:

104. *Qualifications for election*: Subject to the provisions of section 105 of this Constitution, a person shall be qualified for election as a member of a House of Assembly if he is a citizen of Nigeria and has attained the age of 25 years and has been educated up to at least the School Certificate level or its equivalent.

(iii) *Local Government Councils*

299. *Qualifications of Councillors*: Subject to the provisions of section 301 of this Constitution, a person shall be qualified for election as a Councillor if he is a citizen of Nigeria and has attained

the age of 21 years and has been educated up to at least the School Certificate level or its equivalent.

Clearly, from a constitutional perspective, English is the primary language of legislation and governance at all levels of the political process. The elevation of three Nigerian languages, Hausa, Igbo and Yoruba to national official language status remains on paper only. Since in the period 1979 to 1983 when the Second Republic was dismissed by the military "adequate provisions" were never "made therefor" for these languages to be used in the national legislature, there is little basis for optimism that things would be different this time around.

More important for the status of English relative to the indigenous languages are the provisions at the national, state and local government levels that require the equivalent of a high school diploma for legislators. As it is, a pass in the English language is necessary to obtain a School Certificate diploma. Therefore, either by design or by default, "the Constitution has enshrined for the foreseeable future a pass in English at the School Certificate level as the qualification for participation in legislative processes" (Oyelaran 1991: 121).

Like its 1979 predecessor, the 1989 Constitution also makes juridical provisions in relation to language. The provisions are spelled out below:

Fundamental Rights

34.   *Right to personal liberty:....*

(3) Any person who is arrested or detained shall be informed in writing within 24 hours (and in a language that he understands) of the facts and ground for his arrest or detention.

35.   *Right to fair hearing:....*

(5) Every person who is charged with a criminal offence shall be entitled--

(a) to be informed promptly in the language that he understands and in detail of the nature of the offence;...

(e) to have without payment the assistance of an interpreter of his own choice;

(6) When a person is tried for any criminal offence, the court shall keep a record of the proceedings and the accused person or any person authorized by him in that behalf shall

be entitled to obtain copies of the judgement in the case
within 7 days of the conclusion of the case.

By implication, the language of the law is also English: The marginalization of the indigenous languages is evident in that all these provisions "taken together, ...prescribe that no person shall have access to the law or to an interpretation of the law "in a language that he understands" unless and until he is arraigned before the law" (Oyelaran 1991: 113). In the Republic of South Africa, there exists a similar divergence between people's language and public/official language. This divergence creates problems not only in the administration of justice, but also in other areas of political participation. How can people participate when they have been educated under apartheid laws in a home language which is different from the languages of virtually all official documents--Afrikaans and English. While in this instance the motivation might have been different, the effect has been the same. For millions of Africans in South Africa, "The rights of citizenship have been denied them not only through apartheid laws, but also through the language barrier, erected and upheld by the Nationalist government to keep black South Africans 'in their place'" (Oberprieler 1992: 30).

Unfortunately, even the choice of an indigenous language in a multilingual society does not necessarily guarantee justice, unless all citizens share at least a common member of the society's speech repertoire. In Tanzania, for example, Swahili became the official language of the primary courts in 1964. All testimony had to be given in, or translated into, Swahili, and the presiding judge's notes had to be kept in Swahili. In the District or High Courts, however, testimony could be given in either English or Swahili, even though official case records were to be kept in English. As Fred Dubow reports, variations in litigants' facility in Swahili strongly influenced their willingness to use the primary courts. Even with the availability of translators, the potential dangers for litigants who did not understand Swahili (in the case of primary courts) or both English and Swahili (in the case of the High Courts) were grave. There is always the possibility of deliberate or inadvertent misrepresentation. Even where this is not the case, the adoption of a neutral tone by the translator in a law court may prove deadly.

The political objectives behind the language provisions in the Constitutions are clear. At one level, they are all driven by the compelling forces of nationism (the choice of English and "national" languages), and nationalism (the preservation of local cultures by preserving languages, and the development and projection of local languages). At yet another level, they are propelled by hidden group agenda which I will discuss in the next section.

C. Educational Language Policy

Historically, the principal post-independence Nigerian government policy document on language in education, the *National ·Policy on Education* (*NPE*) predates the 1979 constitution. However, it was primarily driven by the same demands of nationism and nationalism. As rightly noted by C. M. B. Brann (1977), work on the NPE was initiated by the post Civil War reality which compelled the federal government to seek an integrative educational policy that could aid the unification process for all the various ethnic and cultural traditions in the country. The government itself makes this motivation quite clear:

> It is Government's wish that any existing contradictions, ambiguities, and lack of uniformity in educational practices in the different parts of the Federation should be removed to ensure an even and orderly development of the country. (*NPE*: 5)

The civil war had brought to the fore the forces of nationalism that had only been pacified by the British and they had nearly torn the country asunder. It was time to begin to seriously nurture nationism rather than taking it for granted. Yet, as would be made obvious in the subsequent discussion, the genie of nationalism could not easily be bottled.

The first public document to formulate language policies was the report of the National Curriculum Conference held in September 1969, titled *A Philosophy of Nigerian Education*. This document provided the guidelines for four subsequent workshops conducted by the Nigeria Educational Research Council (NERC) between 1970 and 1973. These were the Conference on High Level Teacher Training (July 1970), the National Workshop on Primary Education (1971), the Third National Workshop on Teacher Education Curriculum (1972), and the National workshop on Secondary School Curriculum (1973). While the reports of these conferences and workshops did not automatically metamorphose into the *NPE*, they served as testing grounds for many of the ideas which informed the general orientation of the *NPE*, and more importantly, they are historically significant as attempts to come to grips with the educational demands of the nation.

The *NPE* was revised in 1981, but the basic provisions remained the same. The *National Policy on Education* has twelve main sections which address three broad topics: the philosophy of Nigerian education, the major educational levels/areas, and administrative and financial implementation of the policy.

Language is first specifically mentioned in the first section of the *NPE* titled "Philosophy of Nigerian Education":

The importance of Language

In addition to appreciating the importance of language in the educational process, and as a means of preserving the people's culture, the Government considers it to be in the interest of national unity that each child should be encouraged to learn one of the three major languages other than his own mother-tongue. In this connection, the Government considers the three major languages in Nigeria to be Hausa, Ibo and Yoruba. (*NPE* Section 1, paragraph 8)

At the pre-primary and primary levels of education, the policy makes the following provisions:

PRE-PRIMARY EDUCATION

(3)   [Government will] ensure that the medium of instruction will be principally the mother-tongue or the language of the immediate community; and to this end will:

(a) develop the orthography for many more Nigerian languages, and

(b) produce textbooks in Nigerian languages.

...(*NPE* Section 2, paragraph 11)

PRIMARY EDUCATION

(4) Government will see to it that the medium of instruction in the primary school is initially the mother-tongue or the language of the immediate community and, at a later stage, English. (*NPE* Section 3, paragraph 15)

The provisions on primary education above have to be read along with two of the stated general objectives of primary education: (a) the inculcation of permanent literacy and numeracy, and the ability to communicate effectively; [and] (f) giving the child the opportunities for developing manipulative skills that will enable him to function effectively in the society within the limits of his capacity (Section 3, Paragraph 14 (a & b)). But, if a child receives only partial education in his mother tongue and is unable to progress beyond primary school how will he be able to develop permanent literacy and self-education to function in his immediate locality? The policy here, as elsewhere, thus contains the seeds of its own failure.

Whereas the 1977 *NPE* had been silent on the question of language in secondary education, stating only that "In specific terms the secondary school should....(d) develop and project Nigerian culture, art and languages as well as the world's cultural heritage;" (Section 4, Para. 18) and, perhaps taking it for granted that English will continue to be the medium of instruction, the revised 1981 policy makes unequivocal statements about language in secondary education. Although only still implying the continued use of English as medium of instruction, it categorically requires English and two other Nigerian languages as "core subjects" at the junior secondary level:

> In selecting two Nigerian languages students should study
> the language of their own area in addition to any of the three main
> languages, Hausa, Ibo and Yoruba, subject to the availability of
> teachers. (*NPE* Section 4 Paragraph 19 (4))

At the senior secondary level, however, only English and "one Nigerian language" are core subjects. At both levels, Arabic Studies and French are electives.

Finally, although the government declares its commitment to adult literacy, the NPE is silent on whether this will be achieved in the mother tongues/languages of the immediate community, the majority languages, or English. It is reasonable to assume, however, that the first option will be chosen. This is similar to earlier colonial practices.

Once again, these policies reflect an attempt to cope with the competing demands of nationism and nationalism--unity and diversity--as well as individual linguistic rights. At the level of nationism, the government seems to be pursuing a multilingual--specifically trilingual--solution to the national language question: Hausa, Igbo and Yoruba. To cope with the demands of nationalism (state and individual rights), it encourages individuals to be triglottic. According to Brann, "Nigeria is therefore steering towards a national trilingualism (Hausa, Igbo,

Yoruba) and an individual triglossia (mother-tongue, other tongue (community language) and further tongue (English)" (1977: 33). Obviously, this is a chaotic state of affairs.

With English--and to a significant extent the mother tongue or language of the immediate community--there seems to be little problem: there are teachers and the will to learn. This is not to suggest, however, that the practice of using the language of the immediate community is unequivocally guaranteed to succeed. Similar policies of vernacular rationalization at regional levels have been attempted elsewhere in countries with significantly less complicated sociolinguistic profiles, but not without considerable problems. For example, Gambia, 60 percent whose citizens speak Mandingo, and which also has Wolof as the lingua franca of the capital has attempted similar rationalization. Bowcock's survey of school teachers in rural Gambia however found little support for the LIC policy. He quotes a teacher saying that "The idea of different geographical areas for specific tribes and languages is not applicable considering the rate of migration" (1985: 357). Laitin also found this to be among the principal challenges the policy faces in Nigeria. For example, states which provide education in the state language (a.k.a. LIC), such as Cross River State which uses Efik, have made no provisions for teaching linguistic minorities in their own mother tongues. Also government's increasing practice of giving subvention directly to the local governments, thus bypassing state governments, severely circumscribes the states' ability to pursue regional language rationalization.

With the "national languages" the situation is quite different. The Army has tried out the policy in its primary schools since 1974: every pupil had to learn one of the three major languages other than his mother tongue in addition to English which is the sole language of instruction. But as Brann (1977) noted, it has been difficult to find teachers, especially of Hausa. The federal government, apparently in a move to improve the situation in all schools, has decided to withhold recognition for certification from any secondary school whose students fail to study at least one of the three national languages other than their mother tongue (Oyelaran 1991). Although this might encourage the training of the teachers of major languages, punishing schools and pupils who through no fault of theirs are unable to find teachers may ultimately breed additional hostility towards the policy.

There are two other fundamental problems with the policy. The first is political. Given the eternal competition for political power between the three major ethnic and linguistic groups, how does each state decide on which national language to learn? Also, if we read these policies along with the constitutional provisions of the language of the National Assembly, an interesting scenario arises. Since any official communication has to be translated into English, could speakers of other languages beside the three "majority" languages not "free-ride on the English translation, thus eliminating the need to learn any of them?" (Laitin 1992: 124). Even if this scenario were to be somehow avoided, will a group that feels played out in the inevitable political juggling not feel great resentment? And can this not then lead to a resurgence of destructive nationalism? Even more important to the question of individual rights, how fair is it to marginalize the myriad of minority languages in the country? Why should an Efik speaker, for example, be compelled to learn the languages of two masters, one previous (English) and one current (Hausa, Igbo or Yoruba)? By joining language in the perennial political power play, the government might inadvertently be fanning the very flames of disruptive nationalism that it seeks to quench. If, indeed, the ultimate goal as many already suspect is to ensure the elimination of all but one of the three major languages (in this case Hausa) as competitors with English, then the country may be embarking on a course potentially more perilous than that which culminated in the Civil War.

At this juncture, it is pertinent to bring in one more government policy statement with respect to language: the *Cultural Policy for Nigeria* which was launched in 1988. The relevant provisions are as follows:

(i)   Promotion of Culture

4.3.5. The State shall foster the development of Nigerian languages and pride in Nigerian culture.

(ii)   Education (as a Focus of Implementation)

5.1.5. The State shall promote the mother tongue as the basis of cultural education, and shall ensure the development of Nigerian languages as vehicles of expressing modern ideas and thought processes.

5.5. Educational Materials and Book Development

5.5.6. The State shall provide special encouragement to the writing of books in Nigerian languages.

9. General Focus

9.2. Nigerian Languages

9.2.1. The State shall recognize language as an important aspect of culture and a vehicle for cultural expression and transmission.

9.2.2. the State shall promote Nigerian languages at various levels of the educational system. Nigerian languages shall thus serve as media of instruction in all subjects in the early years of primary education with appropriate books being designed and produced in such language for such purpose.

9.2.3. the State shall seek to:

(a) develop technical terms in various fields in Nigerian languages;

(b) develop literacy, post-literacy and other adult education facilities; and

(c) promote the publication of books, newspapers, learned and academic journals in Nigerian languages;

(d) *cultivate a common language for the nation.* (Oyelaran 1991: 128-29)

This policy would seem to be a further articulation of the government's position on language as reflected in the *NPE*. As matter of fact, in respect of the provisions in Paragraph 9.2.3 (a), for example, the national government had already prepared a quadrilingual legislative terminology of over 6000 items in English and the three major languages. The abrupt dismissal of the Second Republic in 1983 did however prevent its implementation (Akinnaso 1989).

In contrast to other policy statements, the *Cultural Policy* declares as a goal "the cultivation of a common language for the nation". This is both puzzling and frightening. Obviously, this cannot be a reference to English, since it is already "common"--at least among the elite. That leaves only the possibility that the intended language is Nigerian, and according to all indications, one of the three "national" languages. This can only spell political disaster and further accelerate the linguistic genocide which the previous policies have already encouraged.

Several people have joined the ensuing debates over the projected language outcome. Recently a statement in support of even the educational policy which encourages language rationalization at the state level by the then Minister of Education, Professor Babs Fafunwa (a principal architect of the Unesco-funded Yoruba Six-Year Primary Project) drew a sharp response from the leading national daily. The *Daily Times* in an editorial not only criticized the minister's position, but also sought to reaffirm the status quo. It wrote:

> The least luxury we can afford in the last decade of the twentieth
> century is an idealistic experiment in linguistic nationalism which
> could cut our children off from the main current of human
> development. (Quoted in Laitin 1992: 123)

With respect to the national language question, there has been a plethora of proposals ranging from the downright silly to the disingenuous. Nwoye (1978) has suggested Hausa or Efik, while Sofunke (1990) rejects the trilingual solution in favor of a single Nigerian language "which can adequately serve as the cultural, political, and linguistic bridge between the cultural North of Nigeria and the cultural South" (1990: 43). It would be interesting to hear his description of what constitutes the cultural North and South as well as the precise point of geographical cleavage between the two. Such references not only make little sense in the light present Nigerian reality, but are decidedly ahistorical. Sofunke suggests Igala, "a Middle-Belt language" for the elevated status of national language. It is from the Middle-Belt, which supposedly constitutes the dividing region between the North and South and is, of course a minority language, a fact that should make it non-threatening, unlike the majority languages, Hausa, Igbo, and Yoruba. One wonders what the other "minorities" in the Middle Belt" would have to say on the choice of Igala.

Laitin suggests a similar role for Pidgin (as an alternative to Hausa, Igbo, and Yoruba) as the lingua franca or "national language" in his projected 3 ± 1 outcome for Nigeria. So does Gani-Ikilama (1990). Elsewhere, I have also raised the possibility of Pidgin English occupying a position in the emerging diglossic situation in Nigeria (Goke-Pariola 1987). Thus, according to Laitin, the individual repertoire would feature English, one of Hausa, Igbo, Yoruba, and Pidgin, a regional language, and for some, a mother tongue or "vernacular". Laitin sees some parallels in other African countries. For example, Lingala which enjoyed widespread usage as a vehicular language in precolonial as well as during the colonial era has been promoted for such a role. It is supposedly the medium of almost 70% of Zairian popular music, is used extensively as a lingua franca in the capital, and in national organizations such as the army, and is strongly supported by President Mobutu Sese Seko and the so-called "Lubumbashi intellectuals" (Bokamba 1976, 1984, Yanga 1980, Laitin 1992).

However, there are significant complications in the Nigerian situation. It is quite true that a lingering suspicion among political scientists and language students is that the trilingual solution to the national language question and the compulsory acquisition of one of the "national" languages in school are only temporary, or stop-gap, measures. The real goal of government--or, at least some powerful group in government--is the ultimate imposition of one indigenous national language. This, apparently through a process of linguistic Darwinism, whereby two of the three languages lose out in the war of attrition, and one becomes dominant within two generations (Brann 1977). As already noted, not a few respectable voices believe this to be Hausa. Even were this scenario to be true, the *Cultural Policy* seems to have taken matters further. It will not allow the nation to arrive at "a common language" through "natural selection"; rather, it will help evolution along the way by eliminating all competitors but one. Such pressures are by no means uniform throughout Africa, even in countries where there is a language which by virtue of its distribution among the populace should be able to dominate all others. For example, it is estimated that as much as 70% of the Zimbabwean population speaks Shona, whereas the nearest rival, Ndebele, is spoken by only 14.6% of the population. Yet, the government has refused to promote Shona as the exclusive national language (Laitin 1992: 134).

The argument behind this cultivation of "one language, one nation", to parody a discredited political party slogan from the Second Republic, is dubious, politically, linguistically, and pragmatically. Throughout human history, several despots have dallied with the idea that a common language is a guarantee of nationism, and that a multiplicity of languages only encourages nationalism. It is true that having a common language may facilitate politically unity, but it has never guaranteed it. One of the most fractious countries in modern Africa, Somalia, for example, is perhaps the only one blessed with not only a single ethnic group, but also an indigenous language--Somali. Serious scholars of language and society as well as political systems will confirm that both unity and diversity are indeed ideologized positions. (See, for example, Fishman 1968a, 1968b, Okafo 1985,

Oyelaran 1988, D'Encause 1978). Even if Nigerians were to suddenly find themselves with one common language, like other people elsewhere they will find other more potent issues to emphasize their nationalism. Certainly, the most serious problem facing Nigeria today is not a national language question.

The selection of the three indigenous languages, Hausa, Igbo, and Yoruba as "national languages" has in effect stratified the national linguistic repertoire, imposing a two-tier Standard Language system with English at the apex, followed by these "national languages". For the several millions of Nigerians who will not be native-speakers of "the chosen tongue" (unless all other languages are legislated out of existence!) the replacement of English with a new "master's tongue", or in the interim, the imposition of new "master's tongues" just after they have started indigenizing the earlier one is unjustifiable, and represents nothing short of linguistic genocide. Their 300 plus languages are condemned to suffer additional social devaluation (All languages already suffer a social devaluation in relation to English). Furthermore, not only does the projected language outcome reflect their weak political power, it also decidedly circumscribes their potential power by limiting the linguistic capital speakers of minority languages can bring to bear upon those crucial markets outside the home domain. Naturally, those who already possess the preferred linguistic capital are at a tremendous advantage when they have to operate in the economic, political, and social market. By employing in addition the usual tools of education and the practical forces of the market place, they would finally succeed in substituting their language as the legitimate competence and their group as the legitimate power.

This fear of marginalization and alienation of minority groups had been articulated even immediately after independence. For example, Chief Anthony Enahoro, an Edo from Edo State (then part of Western Region) made the following statement in the Parliament in 1961:

> ... as one who comes from a minority tribe, I deplore the continuing evidence in this country that people wish to impose their customs, their languages, and even their way of life upon the smaller tribes....My people have a language, and that language was handed down through a thousand years of tradition and custom. When the Benin Empire exchanged ambassadors with Portugal, many of the new Nigerian languages of today did not exist. (Quoted in Allan,

1978: 398).

Besides the implications for power relations, this sentiment validates Laitin's explanation of the psychological dimension to why language outcomes do matter:

> Because symbols evoked by hearing one's own (or a foreign) language have deep psychological resonance among constituents, politicians cannot be merely technocratic about its use. And because people feel that it matters, in an important way it does matter.
> (1992: 50)

Of course, all too often those who articulate language policies that may hurt minorities are not simply technocrats interested in state construction but individuals and groups who are consumed by the desire to accumulate and maintain power for themselves and their groups.

From a pragmatic viewpoint, the projected solution is equally unworkable. Even countries with massive coercive powers have not succeeded in imposing linguistic genocide: it has not worked in the Soviet Union, for example. As Oyelaran (1991) has rightly noted, this dalliance with a common language for Nigeria by the turn of the century or beyond will be nothing but a diversionary undertaking which will not only marginalize a majority of Nigerians, but finally let loose several genies of nationalism that it purportedly seeks to bottle.

Language, it seems, has now finally arrived as a tool in the perennial power play between the various ethnic groups in Nigeria. Constitutional, educational, and cultural language policy statements have now been used as a means of advancing the political agenda of dominant groups at the expense of minorities. But even more interesting, the temporary truce among the majority groups will be shattered by the goal of the cultural policy, which seems to be the first really clear indication of the real nature of this political end game.

D. The Examples of Tanzania and the Republic of South Africa

It is instructive to take a brief look at how some other African countries whose sociolinguistic configurations differ from Nigeria's own have dealt with this issue. Tanzania, which Laitin (1992) groups among those countries whose language outcome will be language rationalization, readily comes to mind. With a population of about 15 million, it has about 100 languages. As noted in Chapter Two, a fortuitous combination of the presence of an African vehicular language, which also cannot be labeled a language of ethnic domination--Swahili--since precolonial times, colonial policies, and ideological orientation of pre-independence and post-independence national leaders has ensured a different process of language legislation in Tanzania, curiously achieving a reversal of the potential power resolution similar to that of the Nigerian and, indeed, other African contexts.

We have already seen how the independence movements in Tanzania, in contrast to those in other African countries elected a language accessible to the generality of the country's 13-15 million citizens as the medium of political organization. Certainly, this was a choice most suited to the egalitarian ideals espoused by Julius Nyerere and his TANU party members. We cannot overstate the fact that the ideological commitment of the nationalist leadership to this egalitarian ideal significantly influenced how language was joined in the struggle for power at the national level. It was certainly not inconceivable that the language of British colonial domination, English, could have been chosen by a different nationalist group committed to a different set of ideological goals and which was more interested in simply assuming the powers and privileges of the country's outgoing colonial masters.

Yet another equally significant observation about the choice of Swahili, beside its being a language of the masses, is that its previous status as an instrument of colonial administration, first by the Germans, and later by the British, has not left any visible taint of colonialism on the language. As William O'Barr rightly notes,

> The fact that first Arab and later European colonialism is primarily responsible for the very wide distribution of the language throughout modern Tanzania tends to be overshadowed by another fact: that it is one of the very few African languages known widely enough to serve major mobilizing and communication roles. (1976: 41)

When Nyerere's party got into office after independence, he moved swiftly to ensure the continued cultivation of Swahili as the national language. Indeed this was considered crucial to the success of the party's brand of socialism. In the period between 1962 and 1965 when the Interim Constitution went into effect, the earlier constitutional provision which stipulated that legislators must be able to read and understand English was naturally set aside. While the new constitution established no linguistic conditions for election into legislative office, it however stipulated that electoral meetings had to be conducted in Swahili. In effect it imposed a language proficiency condition on legislators: all parliamentarians must be fluent in Swahili (Tordoff 1967). In contrast, during neighboring Kenya's 1969 election, the sentiments of Jomo Kenyatta regarding Swahili notwithstanding, prospective parliamentarians had to pass an English proficiency test.

The role of the Tanzanian political leadership in this process of ensuring the success of an African language, Swahili, as a language of nation-building and political access for the masses cannot be overemphasized. The choice of an indigenous language was indeed central to TANU's ideological goals. Among the central objectives of the party, as initially stated by its executive committee were the following:

(a) to prepare the territory for self-rule and to fight for national freedom

(b) to fight tribalism and any other factors which would hinder the development of unity among Africans

(c) to abolish all sorts of segregation

(d) to encourage and help workers establish trade unions. (Kaniki 1974: 1-2, quoted in Abdulaziz 1980)

Consequent upon these egalitarian sentiments, when TANU came into power Swahili was seen as a ready tool which could assist the party to realize its objectives. In 1964, the office of Promoter of Swahili was established to coordinate all activities in support of the nurturing of Swahili's role in state construction and consolidation. Also, as part of the responsibilities of the Ministry of Culture, it promoted the interpretation and translation of dances, songs, and folktales into Swahili. And, in 1967, then Vice-President Kawawa directed that English should only be used in those areas of public life in which Swahili was not yet sufficiently capable of functioning effectively. That same year the Tanzanian government, by an Act of Parliament, established the National Swahili Council. The functions of the Council were:

(a)   to promote the development and usage of the Swahili language throughout the United Republic.

(b)   to co-operate with other bodies in the United Republic

which are concerned to promote the Swahili language and
to endeavor to coordinate their activities.

(c)   to encourage the use of the Swahili language in the conduct
of official business and public life generally.

(d)   to encourage the achievement of high standards in the use
of the Swahili language and to discourage its misuse.

(e)   to cooperate with the authorities concerned with
establishing standard Swahili translations of technical terms.

(f)   to publish a Swahili newspaper or magazine concerned with
the Swahili language and literature.

(g)   to provide services to the Government, public authorities,
and individual authors writing in Swahili with respect to the
Swahili language. (Abdulaziz 1980: 166)

The Arusha Declaration further codified the principles that would guide
Tanzania's brand of socialism. Underpinning this declaration was the principle of
self-reliance. This self-reliance also extended to matters of language, as the
subsequent government statement of principles and also actual practice in the areas
of education, political organization, the civil service, and mass communication
reveal. Most instructive is a statement credited to President Julius Nyerere in the
pamphlet titled *Education for Self-Reliance*. Arguing against the common elitist
educational practices in several African countries which employed European
languages as media of instruction and instead for the integration of education with
national life, he states as follows:

> For the majority of our people the thing which matters is that they
> should be able to read and write fluently in Swahili, that they should
> have an ability to do arithmetic, and that they should learn
> something of the history, values, and working of their country and
> government, and that they should acquire the skills necessary to
> earn their living. (It is important to stress that in Tanzania most
> people will earn their living by working on their own or on a
> communal *shamba*, and only a few will do so by working for wages
> which they have to spend on buying things the farmer produces for
> himself.). (1967b: 24)

Thus, the primacy and success of Swahili in public education was reinforced. We might also add that a similar theory served as one of the bases of the Yoruba Six-Year Primary Project carried out by the University of Ife, in Nigeria. Under the guidance of the Ministry of Culture and Youth's Directorate of National Language the cultivation of Swahili as national language has continued. This Directorate is organized in a way to ensure that its activities permeate to the grassroots level. Besides the office of National Promoter of Swahili, it also has several Regional Language Promoters, District Promoters, and Divisional Language Promoters. In addition, there are public and private language bodies whose activities complement those of the National Directorate of Language (Abdulaziz 1980).

Today, Swahili is not only the national language but the language of education through the secondary level, and it is increasingly being used at the tertiary level as well. No doubt, besides the efforts and vision of Tanzanian political leadership, the fact that it is considered a mother tongue by less than 10% of the Tanzanian population--although current estimates of vernacular-Swahili bilingualism range from 80% (O'Barr 1971, 1976) to 90% (Abdulaziz 1971, 1980)--played no less a role in its evolution as a national language. This is a point often lost on many advocates of other "minority" languages for the role of national language in countries like Nigeria. Without all the other historical factors which have aided the evolution of Swahili in Tanzania such a choice will be doomed to failure. Certainly, the thirty years plus after independence, a bitter civil war, and ongoing occasionally fratricidal political conflicts which have polarized virtually all identifiable "majority" and "minority" groups is not the most opportune moment to make such a proposal and expect even a minimum chance of success. In any case, the ideological and political agenda of the various dominant power groups, ethnic or otherwise, definitely precludes such a language outcome. And they, in particular those affiliated with the Hausa-Fulani groups, are in unquestionable command of the very instruments the state may use to institute language policies.

However, the story of the rise of Swahili to its present lofty heights has not been without its unintended victims. As Jean O'Barr has pointed out, the fact that Swahili is virtually the exclusive medium of political and other public communication has tended to empower males, the young, and the educated. This restriction of participation in the political process, especially at the district level, then, has the tendency to exclude women. As those least likely to go to school and to have an extensive pattern of interaction outside the home--that is, in those places where Swahili is easily acquired by those for whom it is not a mother tongue--many rural women may be victimized. For example, O'Barr claims that at Village Level Councils in Pare district Swahili is used in spite of the fact that "members and constituents tend to have a common tongue, unlike the situation in the district councils" (1976: 80). Therefore, in the conflict between the language of nationism and national egalitarianism (Swahili) and the language of nationalism and local egalitarianism (the vernacular) the latter loses out to the process of rationalization. Perhaps the only saving grace is that this tendency to disenfranchise women, the old, and the less-educated is but an unintentional consequence of the process of state building.

In his review of Tanzania as a case of language rationalization outcome, Laitin recalls the German experience in the country. When after the anti-German Bushiri revolt of 1889-1890 the German government took over Tanganyika from private companies, the new governor set out to use German as the language of administration. However, the Muslim population would only lend him their support, which was considered crucial, if the German government would adopt Swahili as the language of administration. This demand was not based upon any particular love for Swahili as an African language. Rather, as the language in which the Muslims carried out their trade it was considered crucial to the maintenance of their economic and social power. The rest of course is history. If we take this little incident into consideration along with all the other factors which aided the evolution of Swahili, we cannot but conclude that what Laitin has described as "Goals, opportunities, and conflicts of interest" (1992: 33) have determined the language outcome in Tanzania, enabling Tanzanians to distance themselves from the situation which obtains in most of their sister states, and to harness language as a tool for the equalization of power and influence, rather than the opposite.

The Republic of South Africa is yet another African country which offers an interesting and equally important example of the interaction of language, power, and ideology in modern Africa. Given the events of the last couple of years, the questions of language in the national political agenda has assumed new urgency. In a February 27, 1992 article appropriately titled "Lost for Words," the South African publication, *The New Nation*, captures the linguistic dilemma of South Africa today. The articles asks if it is possible "in a country where language has been used for decades as an instrument of oppression--to develop a policy that is not only workable, but helps in the process of reconstruction" (9).

This question is not without good reason. In the 350 years or so of the history of European involvement with that region of Africa, the language question has always been an integral part of the struggle for political hegemony and legitimacy. While in the early days of Dutch occupation of the Cape they relied on interpreters, by the time the Dutch East India Company became entrenched Africans who wanted to work for the company had to learn Dutch (Oberprieler 1992). Subsequently, Dutch contact with Malay and Khoisan slaves led to the evolution of a new language, Afrikaans.

Whereas the emphasis of the original Dutch settlers had been on trade rather than proselytization and education, the advent of the British (1795-1803, and 1806-1814) brought dramatic changes. Indeed, as Roberge has noted, "Afrikaner group consciousness and solidarity find their origin in the 1870s as a reaction to the British imperial factor" (1990: 136). For the first time, the Dutch faced a challenge to their power, as the English language also threatened the hegemony of Dutch. According to Oberprieler, the consequence was the so-called "taalstryd" (language struggle)--which accompanied the protracted Anglo-Boer conflict. The defeat of the Dutch settlers in the Anglo-Boer War of 1899-1902 only served to strengthen Afrikaner nationalism, of which their new language, Afrikaans, served as a focal point. The Second Language Movement (1903-1919), much like the First Language Movement of 1875-1898, sought to give expression to Afrikaner linguistic nationalism the goal of which was to immediately appropriate for Afrikaans those very functions which hitherto had been reserved exclusively for Dutch and English.

The Union of South Africa came into being in 1910, with English and Dutch still the official languages. But when the Afrikaner dream finally came true with the ascension to power of the National Party in 1948, they immediately proceeded to subvert English in favor of Afrikaans both in public and social domains. Where this proved impossible, they sought to ensure that Afrikaans was at least at par with English (Oberprieler 1992: 30). The implication of this policy is that South Africa's population of thirty millions would be served by two languages which were mother tongues to only about 7.7 million people, that is, about 23% of the population. Over the years, the use of Afrikaans spread among other groups and soon became one of the founding pillars of apartheid ideology--*"Ons Taal"* (Our Language). The other two main pillars of apartheid ideology are *"Ons Land"* (Our Land) and *"Ons Volk"* (Our People). The Afrikaners had successfully harnessed linguistic nationalism for the goal of a South Africa united under Afrikaner domination. So powerful is this linguistic pillar of apartheid that only blacks were, and still are, grouped on the basis of language. Race, rather than language, is the basis for the classification of others--whites, in particular. Thus, language is effectively used to affirm one group's legitimacy in power and to deny others any power, not only by separating them from others, but also by separating them (blacks) from one another and fanning nationalistic hatreds:

> This basic concept of apartheid ideology, the equalization of language, culture, and nation, is completely removed from reality and was mainly devised to divide black people in [South Africa] -- an aim which has, unfortunately, been successful to a considerable extent. (Oberprieler 1992: 30)

It is important to note that even the entire history of the evolution of Afrikaans itself as a language has not been free of the larger ideological and power struggles that have characterized the entire history of South Africa's evolution as a nation-state. Paul Roberge's review of the scholarship surrounding the debate about the status of Afrikaans as a language is particularly instructive in this regard. The principal issue in this case is whether or not Afrikaans is a creole language. Whereas outside of South Africa the general view in linguistic circles is that Afrikaans is a semi-creolized variant of Dutch which evolved from contact between Dutch settlers and Asian and African groups, "the creolization model is abhorrent to most Afrikaner scholars, who want to 'see their language white and pure like their race' (Valkhoff 1971: 467)" (Roberge 1990: 133). It is principally for this reason that they allude to the position which I mentioned earlier of excluding the study of the language as spoken by people who are not white, and "have applied the idea of apartheid to the history of Afrikaans in so far as they deal with the Dutch of Europeans, Khoikhoi and slaves (and their descendants) as separate phenomena" (Roberge 1991: 133). Obviously then, what the white Afrikaners and their linguistic brethren most wish to see is an Afrikaans which is but a continuation of white dialects of Dutch.

Linguistic practice in South Africa consequently became but a part of the entire "symbolic universe" which was defined by civil religion as well as social philosophy with the goal of propagating a predetermined (Afrikaner) ideology. According to Roberge, Afrikaner civil religion held that the Afrikaner (much like the Jew of the Old Testament) has been "specially chosen" by God, and given a manifest destiny with a distinctive language, culture, and history. Roberge also cites in support of this thesis the proclamations of a principal advocacy group for this civil religion, the Patriot Movement:

> Typical of its propaganda are calls for 'true Afrikaners' to turn to the language of their hearts, to recognize the mother tongue that God has bestowed upon them. The diversity of peoples and languages is the will of God, who has revealed Himself to individual races in their own languages. Isomorphism between language and people is the divine order of things. (1991: 137)

Working in tandem with this civil religious theme was a social philosophy which stressed the symbiotic relationship between cultural and human relationships. According to the Afrikaner nationalists,

> Language along with race, history, history, fatherland, religion and culture are the defining characteristics of a people. Language reflects a people's character; no nationality could exist without a language. (Roberge 1991: 137)

Of course, the Afrikaner vision of the nation is not one of voluntary association nor of a popularly elected government. After all, it is one divinely ordained. Without the civil religion and social philosophy, others, in particular blacks who spoke Afrikaans even as mother tongue, might have been able to share equally in this ordained heritage. But the combination of linguistic nationalism with Afrikaner social philosophy and civil religion made it possible for race to be appropriated for the purpose of providing an "ethological barrier" to even those who shared with Afrikaners a common linguistic culture. Simultaneously, however, in "forcing the study of Afrikaans upon African schools,...the government bared its underlying determination to secure a new era of Afrikaner dominance" (Marcum 1988: 60). Thus in their linguistic beliefs and practice which reflected the exclusive and racist character of Afrikaner social philosophy, we see a classic example of the use of language as an instrument of power and ideology. We shall soon see how in the last two years Afrikaners have begun to reverse their position, claiming some of these same previously excluded groups, as the threat of a new black-controlled South Africa becomes a distinct, and for many, frightening possibility, thus demonstrating the fact that ideologies, far from being static, do change over time in response to historical pressures.

Currently, there is extensive debate of language policy for "a future South Africa," and the battle lines in the inevitable struggle for power and legitimacy are already virtually drawn. Among those currently clearly discernible positions are those of the people who want English to be the sole official language, those who would keep that position for Afrikaans, and the ANC position in favor of extensive multilingualism.

Central to the ongoing debates is the report of the National Language Project (NLP) in Cape Town, which shows that the project leaders at least have a clear appreciation of the relationship of language to power. In an article titled "Babel rules as official language debate hots up," *The City Press* quotes Nigel Crawhall, NLP organizer for the international conference on alternatives in the language policy of a democratic South Africa. According to Crawhall,

> It is the NLP view that language and power are closely
> related and if the idea of a democratic South Africa is to empower
> all its people, then the language of the people should be central in
> any new language policy... (1991: 10)

In line with this view, the basic assumption which underlies the NLP's report is the equality of all South African languages. The report proposes three models for successive implementation:

1. English as national official language; all other languages, including Afrikaans, will be regional official languages.

2. English, Standardized Nguni, and Standardized Sotho will be the national official languages; other languages will enjoy regional status.

3. Standardized Nguni and Standardized Sotho will be the only national official languages. (Oberprieler 1992: 4)

In this proposed language outcome, both English and Afrikaans will be phased out as official languages.

Predictably, this report has been criticized by several South Africans. The goals of the NLP report are diametrically opposed to the vested interests of groups whose power as well as the dominance of whose ideologies would be directly challenged by its implementation. In a report in its 1 March, 1992 edition, *The Sunday Times* claims that The English Academy of South Africa, for example, contends that English should be the sole official language of a "new South Africa" (5). Also, according to *The Natal Mercury*, Allan Hendrickse, the Labour Party leader, "has thrown his support behind English as the only official language of the future for South Africa" (27 May 1991, p.8). In response to the position of The English Academy of South Africa, FIJ van Rensburg, "special professor in Afrikaans" at the Rand Afrikaans University, claims that there are one million more Afrikaans speakers in South Africa than those who speak English. This, of course, now includes those Coloureds and other Africans who had been previously excluded in the heady days of Afrikaner ethnolinguistic nationalism. He argues what is now considered the "mainstream" Afrikaner position--English and Afrikaans as official languages, with the possible addition of one or two African languages, a solution certain to preserve the power of the present ruling group.

Finally, the African National Congress (ANC) has waded into the debate with a carefully crafted working paper produced by its Language Commission. The most specific statement of the ANC position is to be found in sections of the document *Discussion Document: Constitutional Principles and Structures for a Democratic South Africa* produced by the ANC Constitutional Committee (1991). In making these policy recommendations, the ANC is understandably very careful in stressing the tentative nature of its constitutional and language recommendations:

> The objective of these documents was not to produce blueprints or position [*sic*]. The objective was to assist our people in discussions around constitution-making to enable them to work out for themselves what they want to see in a new constitution and what they would like to see incorporated in a Bill of Rights ...[and] to formulate documents identifying *principles* and a possible *structure* for a new Constitution. (ANC *Constitutional Principles and Structures*, p.2)

The specific language provisions in the document are as follows:

> 9.1.   All languages of South Africa will have equal status. They will be set out in a Schedule to the Constitution and will include in

alphabetical order the following Afrikaans, English, Sipedi, Sesotho, Seswati, Tsonga, Tswana, Venda, Xhosa, Zulu.

9.2.   The State shall take all reasonable and necessary steps to protect, promote and enhance the language rights of all the people of South Africa in relation to education and culture and in the functioning of the State at local, regional and national levels.

9.3.   The language policy of the state shall be directed towards promoting and encouraging multilingualism and preventing the use of any language or languages for the purposes of domination or division.

9.4. The State shall, however, be empowered to make reasonable provision by law for the use of one or more of the languages in different regions of the country, or for specific purposes.

9.5   The question may, of course be asked whether there should be one official language for the country. But if this choice is made it would mean the demotion of some languages or the promotion of a single one. Also, it would mean that the official language would be one which most of the people either do not speak or do not speak fluently.

9.6   It would seem therefore that the most appropriate thing to do is to give equal status to all languages subject to the right of the Government to give primacy to one or more languages in any region or throughout the state as the language of administrative communication or judicial record, or for other purposes throughout the State or in any area. But every one should be entitled to use her or his language for purposes of communicating with the public service. (27-29)

This is obviously an ambitious statement of purpose and intent. The possibly unparalleled length of the language provisions equally bears testimony to a keen sensitivity to the role that language has played in the accumulation and denial of power, and in the legitimation of group ideologies in the process of state construction and consolidation in South Africa. This stands in stark contrast to the situation in neighboring Namibia whose experience has not been much different from that of South Africa. Namibia's Constitution expressly states that "The official language of Namibia shall be English" (Article 3, Section (1)). As the ANC itself states in its policy statement on language in education, "the language question needs to be high on the agendas of all organisations and communities" because "It deals with the tights of people, with questions of power and influence, with issues of access and education, and with the central matters of identity, nationality and unity" (1). Therein also is to be found the source of the policy's potential problems.

Besides statements reinforcing the position of African languages in education and the media, the document *African National Congress Language Policy Considerations* also touches upon the important issue of linguistic capital in the economic market. Noting that, currently, "the language of the employer prevails in negotiations and other central forms of interaction"--a situation which puts workers at a disadvantage--it advocates that "Contracts, instructions, negotiations, notices and rules relating to the workplace and places of living [in mining corporation compounds] should be in a language in which workers and residents are competent" (5). It concludes by reinforcing the ANC's understanding of the ideological nature of language policy and its determination to subvert the status quo and establish a new equilibrium:

> There is no need for people to continue being victims of language
> whereby possibilities are stunted, reality is distorted and judgement
> is warped.

> In particular, the ANC wishes to avoid conditions of linguistic
> privilege with its concomitant gathering of power, influence and
> information in the hands of the elite. ...In a number of African
> countries, the mass of the people does not have access to the
> languages of government, power and influence. As one of the
> means to empowerment, language in South Africa needs to become
> a force which makes every person somebody whose concerns have

to be taken seriously. (6).

Certainly, the ANC has read its country's history well, as well as it has that of Africa and the rest of the world.

From these and other pronouncements of the ANC, the following outcomes seem possible:

1. English only as official language.
2. Six official languages: English, Afrikaans, Nguni, Sotho, Tsonga, Venda.
3. Four official languages: English, Afrikaans, Nguni, Sotho.
4. English only, plus regional official languages.
5. English and Africans, plus regional official languages.

All these options, with the exception of the first, the ANC working paper acknowledges, would be costly financially and in time. And the ANC position has not gone without considerable criticism. For example, the *New Nation* article cited earlier concludes that this proposal "is tailored to satisfy all constituencies rather than [to] provoke constructive debate towards the development of a workable policy" (9). The policy indeed risks prolonging the dominance of English and Afrikaans by default. In a context in which so many national and regional official languages operate and presumably compete (with English and Afrikaans enjoying the advantage of history), the African masses may indeed resort to the classic scenario of "private subversion of public good" by sending their children to schools which use the present languages of domination. After all it was mainly the perceived role of language (Afrikaans) as an instrument of denying opportunity and power which fueled the tragic Soweto riots of 1976. English and Afrikaans may be seen as the ultimate languages of economic opportunity and social mobility. But the dilemma of the ANC is understandable. Not only must it tread cautiously because it does not yet have power, it also must be sensitive to its reading of the role of language in the definition of power and privilege as well as ideology in South African history. It must equally be faithful to its revolutionary ideals of not substituting a new elitism based on language and ethnicity for the old one based on language and race.

E. Conclusion

What has been clear in the different African situations that have been examined, regardless of whether the preferred linguistic competence advocated in policy documents is indigenous African or not, is the centrality of language to the acquisition of power and the imposition of ideologies. In post-revolution 17th century France, power groups aided in part by the social philosophy implicit in Condillac's theory of "the purification of thought through the purification of language" used the concept of "linguistic unification" to accumulate power. In Africa, similar power groups have used the concepts of "authenticity," "language freedom," "separate destinies," "national language," "nationalism," and several others, in pursuit of the same goal: the *de facto* monopoly of power for themselves and their offspring. In this context, then, Africa's situation cannot be said to have been ahistorical.

CHAPTER FOUR

THE SOCIOLOGIES OF LANGUAGE, CULTURE, AND EDUCATION

A. Introduction

So far, I have looked at the evolution of the interplay between language and power in the national polity, especially as can be seen in the language policies adopted by both the colonial and post-colonial governments in Nigeria and some other African countries. However, this provides only an incomplete picture. What it shows, as far as one can determine from explicit statements, is the intention of those in power, whether groups or individuals, and to what extent they are willing to use language as a tool to advance their group's, or the entire nation's, political agenda. What remains to be seen is what the people themselves do with language, perhaps in spite of the various government policies. In other words, what is the situation on the ground, and why is this so?

To some extent, I have addressed this question in the historical context, where I sought to demonstrate that the practice was usually at variance with government's stated policy owing both to pragmatic educational considerations as well as the psychological disposition of the colonized, a state of mind easily explained in terms of the manner of colonization as well as the dominant ideology of colonial capitalism. Now, I intend to shift the focus to the "language situation," that is to say, the total configuration of language use in independent Nigeria--how many and what kinds of languages are currently spoken, by how many people, and under what circumstances, as well as the attitudes and beliefs about languages held by the population.

When we look at the 400 plus languages that constitute the indigenous languages of Nigeria as well as Pidgin and the exogenous languages, English and Arabic, we find significant differences in their use. These differences are in terms of their geographic spread, function, and structural characteristics. Estimates of the spatial distribution of the languages in Nigeria vary. But the figures below represent the generally agreed spatial distribution of the major languages. Hausa (22%) is widely spoken in at least ten of the thirty states in Nigeria. Yoruba (21%) is found in eight states, some of which are virtually monolingual. Like Hausa, it is also to be found among significant populations in other West African countries. Igbo (18%) is spoken in five states, although it has a strong presence in two others.

There are nine other languages which are often considered second-level major languages, basically because they represent majority languages in some states of the federation: Fulfude/Fulani (8.71%), Efik (4.6 %), Kanuri (4.2%), Tiv (2.2%), Ijo/Izon (1.8%), Edo (3.4%), Nupe (1.23%), Igala (1.2%), Idoma (0.9%). Taken together, these major languages are variously estimated to account for between 80 and 90 per cent of mother tongue speakers in Nigeria, while the remaining 380 plus "minority" languages account for between ten and twenty percent of the population.

The functional uses of the various languages, or groups of languages, are determined by a variety of factors. These include government policy, setting, topic, the individual, etc. In discussing the uses to which these various languages are put in Nigeria, I have adopted a mixture of the sociological and social-psychological approaches, both embedded within an anthropological framework. Thus, I will discuss the languages basically in terms of domains but will proceed to interpret the individual language choice in these domains both as a function of individual needs as well as of the larger cultural issue of group or ethnic identity. This chapter will be devoted exclusively to the domain of school, or education, in general. The crucial role that formal education plays in the acquisition of English, and to varying degrees, the mother tongues justifies this selective treatment. Indeed, what happens to the languages in the domain of education is directly related to their fate in all other domains which will be discussed together in the next chapter. Thus, in this chapter I will discuss how the sociology of language relates to the sociologies of education and culture in African nations. Again, I will use the Nigerian example to illustrate the consequences of this relationship. I consider this chapter particularly crucial in that it demonstrates the practical classroom consequences of language policy and language use.

B. Language and Education

Education, or the school domain, seems a most appropriate point at which to begin this discussion for several reasons. First, language use in education has been the object of state legislation virtually since the beginning of formal education in Africa. It also gives us a clue as to where the country may be headed in terms of language use both within and outside the country itself. Finally, quite apart from serving as a barometer against which to measure the success or otherwise of government policy, it also provides a reliable indication of how the individual positions himself in relation to the multidimensional universe of discourse in which he finds himself.

Perhaps more important is the role that education plays by its ability to facilitate the imposition of sanctions on those who deviate from what has been defined as the legitimate competence, or the desired legitimate competence. In the Nigerian and other African contexts, education has certainly been harnessed for the purposes of prosecuting the direct and indirect struggles of various interest groups for power and hegemony.

The relative power of English and other erstwhile languages of colonial domination in Africa is directly contingent upon the role of education as the key to elite status. One of the things which educational systems do is to define the "legitimate language". In the Nigerian case, it is clearly English. All other varieties of speech are consequently subject to sanctions which are either externally imposed (by the authorities and the reality of the market, for example) or they are self-imposed. As Bourdieu notes,

> The laws of the transmission of linguistic capital are a particular case of the laws of the legitimate transmission of cultural capital between the generations, and it may therefore be posited that the linguistic competence measured by academic criteria depends, like other dimensions of cultural capital, on the level of education (measured in terms of qualifications obtained) and on the social trajectory. (1991: 61)

Hence our apparent inability to separate either the sociology of culture or the sociology of language from the sociology of education.

Besides functioning as the institution with the delegated authority to inculcate a uniform set of linguistic skills, the school is also characterized by a tendency to vary the intensity, and the length, of this process in accordance with the students' inherited cultural capital. Even though there is no well-defined social stratification in Nigeria and several other African countries yet, students from poor and non-urban middle class families are placed at a disadvantage since they are least likely to go to school, or stay long enough to acquire the linguistic capital so necessary for success in the markets outside the school. This is generally true of all societies, as Bourdieu's argument clearly demonstrates:

> ... As a linguistic market strictly subject to the verdicts of the guardians of legitimate culture, the educational market is strictly dominated by the linguistic products of the dominant class and tends to sanction the pre-existing differences in capital. The combined effect of low cultural capital and the associated low propensity to increase it through educational investment condemns the least favoured classes to the negative sanctions of the scholastic market, i.e. exclusion or early self-exclusion induced by lack of success... those least inclined and least able to accept and adopt the language of the school are also those exposed for the shortest time to this language and to educational monitoring, correction and sanction. (1991: 62)

The post colonial situation in most African societies clearly supports Bourdieu's thesis.

One of the most glaring and profound contradictions that characterize post-colonial states in Africa is the existence of nominal political independence alongside economic, cultural, and psychological dependency on the foreign cultures and powers--East (at least until most recently) and West. For this, the inherited educational system and philosophy are largely responsible. Education has been artificially separated from the overall socioeconomic, political and cultural development of peoples and nation states.

Given the political economy of the colonial state as discussed in Chapter Two, the overall objective of colonial education as practiced by churches and successive colonial administrations was very simple: It was to ensure that the colonizers and the various public services could meet their requirements. This explains why, for example, it was never considered necessary to educate the masses, after all "only a minority of the [African] population entered the colonial economy in such a way that their performance could be enhanced by education" (Rodney 1974: 257). The school curriculum promoted the colonizer's culture, history, religion, and ways of life. Colonial education, or perhaps, miseducation, sought in addition to inculcate the values of docility, humility and faithful acceptance without question, all qualities considered necessary in the colonized for the sustenance of colonialism.

The recovery of political independence notwithstanding, the problems and contradictions of colonial education continue to be felt throughout the continent and indeed the entire "Third World". It is in this regard that Mugomba and Nyaggah (1980) cite the pertinent observation of the Development Education and Development and Peace in Canada to the effect that:

> Educational systems in the ex-colonies remain largely intact [long]
> after independence. Curriculum, language [of instruction], and, in
> some cases, even the nationality of the teachers, are carried over
> from the colonial period. (3)

The significance of language (of instruction), and we might add the pedagogy, in this process of continued sociocultural and psychological dependence cannot be overemphasized. As the principal vehicle of culture and the handmaiden of formal education, its pedagogy becomes crucial. As will be demonstrated shortly, the use of English in Nigerian education has only aided the above process. Literacy pedagogy reinforces rather than challenges the existing patterns of psychological, economic and political dependence on the West.

Adebisi Afolayan (1979), although by indirection, perhaps best summarizes the situation of language use in education today when he writes:

> There is politics [in Nigeria] without English. There is trade without
> it. Administration takes place at the local level without it. But there
> can be no pretence at formal education wherever and whenever
> English cannot be used as the medium of instruction or at least
> taught as a subject. (14)

This importance is reflected through all levels of education in Nigeria, as we shall see in the examination of language policy instruments and their implementation.

B.1. Pre-Primary and Primary Education

According to the *National Policy on Education* (*NPE*), education at the pre-primary level as well as in the first three grades is supposed to be given in the mother tongue or the language of the immediate community. The practice however has been radically different. For one thing, most patrons of the relatively few pre-primary institutions are middle class and upper class parents concentrated in the urban areas. One demographic feature of urban centers is their extremely diverse linguistic composition. Given this fact then, it becomes obvious that the mother tongue/language of the immediate community policy cannot work here. Many of the parents do not speak the local language, and the children would still be too young to have acquired the language. Therefore, for pragmatic reasons English has remained the major, if not the exclusive, language of instruction.

One other consideration is the availability of teaching material in the local languages. Even where it might be feasible to use a local language, such use will be non-structured, but rather incidental. There is simply very little available in form of books and other learning aids for the preschool child in the local languages. In the nursery schools that I have visited (1989) in Kaduna, Lagos, Ile-Ife, Osogbo and Ibadan, for example, the pre-school books I saw were not only written in English but published in Britain. One of the most popular was the "Ladybird" series, which is British. Even when teachers depart from the written text, the oral teaching is in form of jingles, which are in English. Consequently, what the kids learn are English nursery rhymes. It might not be overstating the case if one were to suggest that should members of the 1922 Phelps Stokes Commission visit a typical urban day-care/pre-school center today, they would be compelled to make the same comments as they did almost a century earlier. I will return to the significance of this state of affairs shortly.

One final factor which significantly affects the language choice and use at the pre-primary level is the psychological predisposition of the middle and upper class patrons themselves. Linguistic handicaps aside, most parents see English as the key to the future. Like the Sierra Leonean parents of over a century earlier, the reason the kids are in school is not to learn more of their own language or culture, or "to make a smooth transition to the primary school"; it is to get a head start in the education game. And any fool knows that English, and no other language, is the key. It is clear, then, that most of these parents will understandably not tolerate anything that they could perceive as diverting their children from the goal of mastering English as early as possible.

Indeed, other African countries display similar examples of this classic example of what Laitin (1992) has aptly described as the "private subversion of public good". In Kenya, for example, this contradiction has pitted the government against parents. The government's language curricula positions could be described thus: (a) English only; (b) Swahili only; (c) English medium, with compulsory Swahili; (d) Vernacular medium, as a bridge to English medium at higher levels. In contrast, the implied position of parents has been (a) Learn English at all costs; (b) Encourage development of vernacular, but use English as a Language of Wider Communication (LWC); (c) Accept national values and assimilate into a Swahili-speaking environment (Laitin 1991: 109). As a consequence, in most schools where in accordance with the government's policy Swahili is taught, most children and parents do not take it seriously. This is a reaction based not simply on parents' preferences, but one also determined by their reading of the government's position. Whereas in the school system "Swahili is a compulsory subject (reflecting the nationalist desire to have an indigenous lingua franca)...success in Swahili has not been necessary for job promotion (reflecting the bureaucratic belief that Swahili is not to be taken seriously)" (Laitin 1992: 113). The Somali elite, Laitin also observes, displays a similar reaction, while in the Cote d'Ivoire, parents pursue French competence for their children in preference to that in the vernacular. The support for a national language here as elsewhere is present, but diffuse, whereas in parent's personal choices they vote in a way that subverts the publicly stated support for a national language. The market value of languages thus determines the success or failure of government policies. Why, indeed, would anyone accumulate a capital that has little or no surrender value?

It will also not be far-fetched to suggest that many parents in fact judge the quality of the pre-school according to how Westernized it is, and the degree of "Englishness" is to them a clear measure of that standard of success. A few years back, there was an apocryphal joke making the rounds of Lagos that your child's pre-school cannot be deemed to have done a good job until your three-year old infant comes home and can say to you : "Don't be silly, daddy," just like a good

English or American child. I believe the point needs no further elaboration.

One might wonder where the government stands in all these. Quite apart from the obvious fact that as elite members of society the government officials are themselves deeply involved as parents and patrons in this deviation from government policy, there are administrative and fiscal problems in its implementation. For one thing, the government simply has far too limited resources to monitor what is going on in the myriad of pre-primary schools, many of which are not even registered with the government. Also, the government does not fund pre-primary education, which limits its ability to interfere in their running. If these are private schools which do not award certificates in need of government recognition, it is doubtful that the government will be in any position to effectively ensure compliance with its policy. Such policy, then, remains largely no more than an exhortation to the schools and parents to "do the right thing" for their children and their cultures. But, obviously, the government and parents hold quite divergent views on just exactly what "the right thing" is, or how to go about doing it.

The problems of language use at the primary school level are basically those of needs and pragmatism. The government policy remains to use the mother tongue for the first three years, and English subsequently. Again, this sounds much like the policy going as far back as the late 1920s. The practice has however varied from this. In some schools, especially in rural areas, the mother tongue is used for the entire six years of primary school. For example, as a Youth Corper in the northern removes of the then North Central State (now Katsina State) in 1975, I found that most of my first-year pupils at the teachers college had been taught in Hausa all their life. They had tremendous problems following the English lessons and, in fact, some teachers continued to use Hausa as a supplementary language of instruction in the school. On the other hand, I found that English was the medium of instruction from the first grade in several schools in Kaduna, then the state capital, as well as in Zaria. This mirrors the situation in virtually all areas of the country.

It may seem ironic that English would predominate in pre-schools and the mother tongue in the primary. But if we understand that nursery schools have largely remained an elitist business where, especially with the Universal Primary Education (UPE) introduced in the mid 1970s, primary education has been for the poor classes as well as the middle and upper classes, then the situation becomes somewhat clearer. There has of course also been the problem of producing enough teachers who themselves are literate in their mother tongue and know it well enough to teach subjects like Elementary Science. In several schools where English is used as sole medium of instruction from first grade it is simply a response to the linguistic mix of the urban areas. Of course, for much the same reason as do their pre-primary counterparts, private primary schools use English virtually exclusively.

B. 2. English in the Secondary School Classroom

The secondary schools offer a most interesting and often troubling scenario in terms of language use. Because of the significance of the secondary school in the three-tier educational system, especially in the production of the educated middle class whose identity is a central concern of this study, I will discuss at length not only the use of language, but its pedagogy as well. Such analysis is critical to a proper apprehension of the subsequent discussion of the interplay of language, power, and ideology in the larger society.

One might begin by saying that until the recent government policies discussed in the preceding chapter the Nigerian languages occupied a very low status in relation to English. Even though they still do not compare with English in prestige and functional distribution, they do not at least suffer from official second-class status and treatment as they did in the period immediately after independence.

The preeminence of English in the secondary schools was considerably facilitated not just because it was the language in which the books were written but by the boarding school system which prevailed then. Although most of the schools were homogenous and those which were not had students who often spoke the local language, the use of the mother tongue was virtually prohibited in the schools. Anyone who had the linguistic misfortune of having gone to school between 1960 and sometime in the early seventies would remember how many times they had been punished for "speaking vernacular" in school. A favorite punishment meted out by the occasionally sadistic senior students who enforced the rules was the infamous "imposition". One of my most enduring memories of my first and, fortunately, only year in the boarding school was writing out the sentence "I will never speak vernacular again in school" 500 times, because I was a repeat offender! For years after I had left boarding school I still had nightmares about this. Yet, my fate pales in comparison to that of my mates who having come from homes where no English was spoken (I was "fortunate" that my father had been to college and was in fact a schoolmaster) and whose wretched tongues would simply not stop forming the words of their "vernacular".

Of course, all who have suffered second class status often manifested in linguistic prejudice or genocide against their group are quite familiar with this scenario. For example, the situation compares in some respects with that of the Irish after the Act of the Union was passed in 1803. In the hands of English administrators, education was redefined to read "learning English". And, in the worst period of their subjugation, many Irish came to believe that the English way of life and language was the only key to social advancement. Thus, the schools embarked on a process not unlike that described above:

> What has been called "the mass flight from the Irish language" was enforced in the national schools by a series of frightening educational measures. Gaelic-speaking children were punished with wooden gags, and subjected to mockery and humiliation. Brothers were encouraged to spy on sisters. Under the regime of the tally-sticks, the child would wear a stick on a string round its neck. Every time the child used an Irish Gaelic word, the parents would cut a notch in the wood. At the end of the week, the village schoolmaster would tally up the notches and administer punishment accordingly. (McCrum *et al* 1986: 183)

What makes the Nigerian situation perhaps more galling though is that Nigeria was at least supposed to be independent, and that the rules were enforced by those whose mastery of the English language was itself at best often dubious.

Thus, in a supposedly independent Nigeria, indigenous languages continue to suffer social devaluation. More than thirty years after independence, and over a hundred years since English was first systematically introduced into the national speech repertoire, Nigerian teachers and scholars have failed to reach agreement on the concept of a Nigerian English. Even though they themselves for the most time do not speak the "Queen's English," several teachers and scholars continue to mark students down for using "Nigerianisms"--that is, whenever these self-appointed guardians of the "Queen's English" can recognize such usage. Many of them suffer from what the Nobel laureate, Wole Soyinka, in a different but pertinent context has described as "externally induced fantasies of redemptive transformation by an alien master".

In what is fast becoming a pronounced diglossic situation, one can posit the argument that English occupies the position that the Standard Language does in relation to other speech varieties (languages, in the case of Nigeria and other similar African countries). This observation is particularly significant because, as Bourdieu correctly argues,

> To speak of *the* language, without further specification, as linguists do, is tacitly to accept the *official* definition of the *official* language of a political unit. The language is one which, within the territorial limits of that unit, imposes itself on the whole population as the only legitimate language, especially in situations that are characterized in French as more *officielle* ... Produced by authors who have the authority to write, fixed and codified by grammarians and teachers who are also charged with the task of inculcating its mastery, the language is a *code*, in the sense of a cipher enabling equivalencies to be established between sounds and meanings, but also in the sense of a system of norms regulating linguistic practices. (1991: 45)

Thus, we understand the task which teachers and scholars see themselves as performing. For them, the need to question the very legitimacy of this Standard does not even arise. Of course, this means that they completely ignore the social conditions surrounding the acquisition of this narrowly defined competence and the condition of the market in which this definition of the legitimate has been established and is being maintained. Their business is simply to teach "good English". It is also easy to understand why there is no obvious resentment on the part of the consumers--students and their parents: the dominant competence does indeed function as linguistic capital, securing "a profit of distinction" in relation to other competencies.

Today, students are, hopefully, no longer punished or reprimanded for speaking their mother tongue. I suspect though that the censorship is now often self-imposed and group-monitored as students struggle to climb up both economically and socially. The rules of discourse notwithstanding, English still is the pre-eminent language in secondary schools. It remains the sole medium of instruction and examination. And no matter how good a student is in his mother tongue and other school subjects he cannot be certified as having successfully completed his secondary education without at least a pass in English. And the 1989 *Constitution* reinforces this status by insisting on this certificate as a pre-qualification for elective office and appointment to ministerial and other offices by elected officials:

> Since the Constitution is a republican instrument of government and elected office holders in the executive branch are free to appoint any member of the citizenry into executive positions, the Constitution further explicitly proscribes the appointment of any person who fails to meet the same conditions [as elected officials] into positions at any level (See Sections 144(5), 148(4), 288, *et passim*). (Oyelaran 1991: 123)

Now, to the matter of the pedagogy of English at the secondary level of the educational system. The pedagogy of English at this level clearly shows how the power distribution is organized via language, between the country and the rest of the world, and how ideology is taught through language. Here, I will seek to illustrate this through the answers to the following three questions:

1. What is the sociocultural significance of the choice of reading passages and essay themes in English language textbooks?

2. Do these passages and essay themes give students the opportunity to explore their historical and cultural past and present?

3. Do the comprehension passages and essay topics encourage students to reflect upon their socioeconomic and political reality? (A passage or theme is political if it highlights power relations, whether sociologically, economically, or institutionally determined).

The distribution of passages and themes as well as how they are presented in the texts give sufficient clues to determine the answers to these questions. The following report by the Africa Research Group of Cambridge, Massachusetts on American intervention in Nigeria indeed seems to underscore the importance of what goes on in the classrooms:

Grooming the Middle Class

A survey of all the imperialist agencies operating in Nigeria--from the Ford Foundation to the A.I.D program--shows that they are concentrating their major resources on building and staffing an educational system to train the middle class. Simultaneously, they are erecting the institutions to employ them and to manage their lives. Francis X. Sutton, now Deputy Vice President of Ford's international division, explains the goals of capitalist internationalism this way:

> If one may venture to use the term stirring unpleasant connotations, it may be said that the Foundations have an important role in linking the modernizing elites of the world. Collaborative efforts in developing assistance and higher learning foster a network of professionals and personal contacts throughout the world.

The foundations and government agencies have coordinated their efforts in this campaign. While Ford provided a team of experts to write Nigeria's first 6-year development plan, A.I.D. promised over $200 million for its financing...This exercise is referred to in social science jargon as "institution building," which itself comes under the heading of "nation building". Education plays a crucial role in the organization of the market as colony. It can no longer be thought of simply as a process of acculturation or ideological training; it now operates within a specific context where it serves a manifold technical function. Without mass education the market system of the corporations cannot function effectively either in terms of the jobs it creates or the consumption patterns it establishes. The process begins at an early age and has a long range effect: Virtually all schoolchildren--in urban areas at least--are dressed in shirts and shorts or dresses. These children comprise an immediate market for children's and teenage clothing, and for European clothing of all sizes in the future. (Chinweizu 1975: 335, 338)

Even as early as the high school years, students are themselves initiated into this cycle of consumerism and the perception of civilization as Westernization. A brief analysis of the most widely used textbooks in high schools illustrates how the use and the pedagogy of English at this level encourages dysfunctional and alienating education, perpetuates neocolonialism, and stunts the students' cultural growth.

The books reviewed here are the *Practical English* (PE) series (Books 1-5) and the *Effective English* (EE) series (Books 1-5). In both series, each book corresponds to a year of high school in the old secondary school system.

Even though the PE books are written by Africans (one Nigerian and one Ghanaian), there is a surprisingly limited number of comprehension passages which have an African background (Passages are classified as African (non-Nigerian), Nigerian, Non-African, and General (e.g. scientific texts)). In fact, of the total of 138 passages, almost 50 percent are non-African (See Table 1 below):

BACKGROUND

Book	African	Nigerian	Non-African	General	Total
PE 1	6	6	16	2	30
PE 2	2	8	19	1	30
PE 3	7	8	7	8	30
PE 4	6	3	14	1	24
PE 5	7	6	11	-	24
Total	28	31	67	12	138
% of Total	20.28	22.46	48.55	8.70	100

Table 1. Distribution of reading passages according to background in the PE books.

It is significant to note that most of the non-African passages are from Western European and North American sources. They are folk tales and excerpts from books such as *Alice in Wonderland,* Jules Verne's *Journey to the Centre of the Earth,* R. L. Stevenson's *Kidnapped* and *Treasure Island,* and Stanley Weyman's *A Gentleman of France.* It should be noted, also, that several of these books are introduced in the first two or three years of high school.

Table 1 shows that less than 23 percent of all the reading passages in the PE series reflect a Nigerian background. Even if we were to add up those texts with Nigerian and other African backgrounds, the total of 46.6 percent still falls below that of Non-African texts (48.5%).

Implicit in this distribution pattern is an assumption that the experience of the students and their society at large is not important; those which are non-

African are infinitely more desirable. If this is the case, then the literacy in English which students develop cannot but alienate them from the society in which they live. Contrary to the goals of both the educational and cultural policies discussed in the preceding chapter, it must also encourage an acculturation to a foreign, Non-Nigerian and non-African world.

Further scrutiny of those passages classified as "Non-African" is illuminating: they are overwhelmingly Western. The only exception in PE 1, "The Arab Doctor," for example, focuses on the Westerners in the story and displays a condescending, Western attitude to non-Westerners. All 14 non-African passages in PE 4 are Western and only 1 of the 11 in PE 5 is not. This is clearly a perpetuation of colonial ideology: any mediation with the rest of the world at all must be through Western eyes.

Even some of the African passages are uncomplimentary to Africans. A passage on lions discusses the life of the Masai of East Africa. It however gives no indication that this way of life belongs in the past. The title is deceptive: the passage is not really about lions but about the "wild African," with the Masai as examples. The hypocrisy of the title becomes evident when we examine another text about animals which is set in Australia. The passage about kangaroos is quite factual; it describes the behavior of the kangaroo in its habitat. A passage like that on lions perpetuates in the minds of learners the picture of the whole of Africa as but one extensive wild-game reserve.

Passages that deal with politics and war also reinforce the suggested irrelevance of local history. A passage in PE 2 deals with politics, but only "in a country where long ago, many parties were struggling for power". The politics of Nigeria, past or present, is irrelevant and unworthy of examination. Yet another text talks about wining the war against the Nazis. It is strange that passages about wars in Africa, if not Nigeria, are not used as well--the Mau Mau struggles against the British in East Africa, the wars of liberation in Angola, Mozambique, Zimbabwe, etc.

The important and heroic struggles of humankind seem to take place only in other parts of the world. Hence, the students learn about the defeat of the Nazis who had killed six million Jews, but nothing about the millions of Congolese the Belgians exterminated early this century. In this same vein, in a passage titled "A Wonderful Discovery," some men "went to an unknown part of South Africa...".

We might ask, unknown to whom? Through such passages, the idea of Africa and the rest of the non-Western world being "discovered" is peddled to students without comment. The unfolding of national history is to be interpreted along Western lines. Other books in the series display similar characteristics. Europeans remain the fighters against some form of tyranny or the other, but never the tyrants against whom others fight. Of all the people mentioned in a passage about "reformers," only Mahatma Ghandi is not a Westerner. Naturally, there is no single African, past or present, who deserves the epithet "great". Similarly, not one African religion qualifies to be one of the "great religions" of the world.

The kind of questions usually asked of students after passages, African and non-African, which at least have the potential to be used critically do not help matters. In PE 4 for example, there is a passage about the British 'explorer' Mungo Park. In the story, the local chiefs who are suspicious or him and did not believe that he and others had come to Africa just for sight-seeing are held up to ridicule and the question of motives is left untreated. It would have been useful to ask, with the benefit of hindsight, whether the chiefs or the gullible subjects were right. Another excerpt, this time from Mugo Gatheru's *Child of Two Worlds*, praises "the fair-mindedness and friendliness of liberal British people [who] impressed me [the writer] very highly, in particular by their courtesy". There are no questions about why if they were so liberal and friendly they colonized, enslaved, and refused to grant independence to many countries at the time of writing and continued to elect governments that supported racism in South Africa are not addressed.

Even within the passages which are Nigerian, there is an obvious problem of balance between various ethnic groups. Most passages are biased in favor of the three dominant political groups or alliances: the Hausa-Fulani, the Yoruba, and the Igbo. The assumption here can only be that the life of minorities is insignificant. Minority students therefore undoubtedly suffer a double alienation. The stated aim of the books in the series is to "attempt to teach English on the modern principles which are rapidly gaining ground throughout the African continent and which have recently been adopted by the West African Examinations Council..." (PE 3: x). The tragedy of assuming that you can teach language without teaching culture or world view in these circumstances is especially tragic. The power differential between local culture and that behind the English language calls for a more critical approach to language teaching.

In this regard, it is particularly important to have material that would teach students about their past. A people that have undergone the traumatic and humiliating experience of colonization during which a great part of their culture has been lost and their history distorted need to relearn their past. Lacking an objective and true apprehension of their history, students are unable to take a decision against history. And yet, the praxis of a liberating education which is crucial for a developing country involves the transformation of the present in order to create a future through an objective apprehension of the past--a past which, of course, cannot be changed, but must be understood to create a better tomorrow. Chinua Achebe characteristically put the matter simply when he said "We must know where the rain began to beat us". And Africans cannot begin to know this if they continue to believe that their African past was "one long night of savagery from which the first Europeans came to rescue [them]".

The specification of essay themes similarly presents a dismal picture. In general, the composition topics in the PE series neither ask the students to use a knowledge of their own culture nor provide the opportunity for reflection upon their sociocultural and political reality. Many simply ask students to perform mechanical tasks of little significance.

Frequently, when students are asked to examine some aspect of their life or community, the audience is foreign. This is the case in three of four such instances in PE 1. In PE 2, four out of five instances are oriented to a foreign audience, while in PE 3 all four such essays are addressed to a similar audience. The usual format is to ask that students write to an 'overseas pen-pal', as the following excerpts show:

1.   Write one paragraph telling an overseas pen-friend about story-telling in your home, saying who tells the stories, to whom, when, where, etc. Say what kind of stories are told but do not tell any story in full. Tell the truth. (PE 1: 19)

2.   Write a letter to an imaginary pen-friend in a foreign country to tell him (or her) about the district in which you live. Include the following paragraphs, and set out your work like a real letter:

1) The general appearance of the district, mentioning hills, rivers,

vegetation, crops, etc.

2) Description of the roads, villages and towns.

3) The people, their houses and occupations. (PE 2: 60)

3.   Imagine you are telling an overseas friend about the wild life...of your country. Do not mention all the animals you know, but say something about the commonest or most interesting ones, and give your own experience where possible.

Write the following paragraphs:

1) Fierce animals.

2) Other animals you know of including those sometimes caught for their meat.

3) Snakes, both harmless and poisonous. (PE 2: 69)

4.   Write a letter to an overseas pen-friend to describe what you know of schooling in this country. Mention the different sorts of school, age and sex of pupils, lessons, hours of work, holidays, language of instruction, etc., illustrating the facts from your own experience where necessary. (PE 4: 221)

These assignments are set up in a manner which could suggest to the students that their community is only worth examining in relation to "overseas," since the questions place students exactly in a situation where what is significant is in relation to "overseas". Others like the third excerpt above draw on stereotypes of the neo-Tarzan kind about what is interesting about Africa; we may ask how many students actually go about thinking of "fierce animals" (except for snakes) much less actually see one.

Other assignments which avoid the ubiquitous pen-friend still orient students towards an overseas country or environment. Where they do not, they set up a rural-urban conflict. In PE 2 for example, students are assigned the following writing task:

Imagine that you have been given just enough money to take you to another country for three weeks during the next holidays, travelling by air. Describe in detail how you intend to get there and what you will do, as follows....

> The class should if possible be informed of an exact air-route, or at
> least of a possible air route, e.g. to New York via Monrovia and
> Dakar. (181)

Nothing is intrinsically wrong with asking students to imagine traveling. However, they are not asked about traveling within their own country first. Here, the students' reality is constructed in such a way as to make the exploration and enjoyment of their own world undesirable, and that of "overseas" the real thing.

In yet another assignment, students are asked to write to a foreign newspaper about "African Dancing". The very concept of "African dancing" is largely foreign and a carry-over from colonialism. While dance styles in many parts of Africa may have similarities, one can hardly make such wide generalizations about them. The theme, therefore, only reinforces the colonial assumption that glosses over the rich variations which exist within the continent. Students are to accept this assumption without question.

Illustrative of the occasional rural-urban conflict that is encouraged is an assignment about movies in PE 3:

> Imagine that an Indian girl of your own age [15-18 years] has
> advertised in a newspaper for a pen-friend in your country who is
> interested in the cinema. Write her a letter to tell her what you
> know about films and the cinema setting our the letter properly and
> dividing it into paragraphs...(57)

The fact is that unless a student lives in an urban center--and few do--he or she is not likely to have seen any cinema house, much less a movie. Even the mobile cinema that was once available and which allowed rural people to see some movies (although they were invariably "cowboy and Indian" films), is now out of service. Therefore, besides its orientation to a foreign audience, the theme is potentially alienating to a majority of students who live in rural areas: it requires them to draw upon an experience which is not theirs.

At other times, the authors seem to have magically taken a trip to a country totally different from theirs. How else is one to explain the rationale behind the following assignment:

> One month ago, you bought a bicycle in a nearby town, paying
> cash. Now the store has sent you a bill for the bicycle. Write a short
> letter to the firm, returning the bill and pointing out that you have

paid for the bicycle, though unfortunately you haven't kept the receipt...(PE 3: 240)

This is a situation in which virtually no Nigerian student can find himself. How can such a mistake arise when stores do not sell their goods to individuals on credit? A similar example is found in PE 4:

Imagine that you recently sent your wristwatch to be repaired under guarantee. It came back satisfactorily repaired, but with half the leather strap missing. The reference number on the accompanying slip was A/231/4. Write:

1) A short letter to the watch company asking for the rest of the strap.

2) The watch company's short reply to accompany the new leather strap, sent free...

(*Footnote*: As well as writing to a firm to enquire about their goods or to order and pay for them, we may wish to return them by post for repair or replacement. This is particularly common when we have bought something, e.g., a watch. 'under guarantee', i.e., the watch is guaranteed to work well for, say, one year, and if anything goes wrong during that time, it will be repaired free, or at specifically low rates. Large firms can usually be relied on to give good and prompt service through the post. Some, called 'mail order' firms, sell all their good through the post after advertising them in the press. (222)

This footnote certainly cannot be describing Nigeria. The kind of service it describes is virtually non-existent, and no student will send his or her watch by post to a firm for repair, assuming the firm even agrees to honor the terms of the guarantee. Furthermore, firms do not sell their goods by mail order. With assignments like this, students cannot but conclude that writing is irrelevant to real life experiences, at least where their own are concerned. Surely, better ways can be found to design assignments which would give students practice in the art of writing business letters without making their experiences irrelevant.

Even though the principal author is an Englishman, the books in the *Effective English* (EE) series include a surprisingly large number of comprehension passages with a local setting. The comparative figures for texts from different backgrounds in all five books in the EE series are given in Table 2:

		BACKGROUND			
Book	African	Nigerian	Non-African	General	Total
EE 1	4	18	2	1	25
EE 2	2	17	5	1	25
EE 3	8	11	2	4	25
EE 4	15	6	6	1	28
EE 5	4	2	3	5	14
Total	33	54	18	12	117
% of Total	28.20	46.15	15.39	10.25	100

Table 2. Distribution of Reading Passages according to background in all five EE course books.

In contrast to the figure of 23% for the PE series, fully 46% of the passages in the EE series reflect a Nigerian setting. Together with the African (but non-Nigerian) passages, they constitute about 74% of the comprehension passages. Again, this contrasts with the lower figure of 46.6% for the PE series. Only 15.3% of all passages in the EE series, compared to 48.5% in PE, have a non-African background.

The higher percentages of passages with a local background is however often misleading. Since many of them are bland, containing nothing of sociocultural significance, the series itself then is not free of the problems of the PE series. For example, some texts also equate the students' social reality with that of their European counterparts. As in the earlier series, Columbus "discovers" the West Indies, just as some other European explorers "discovered West Africa" (EE 2). A unit titled "The Story of Nigerian Groundnut" concentrates on the uses to which the British put the groundnut. Nothing is said about the uses in Nigeria before and after the British arrival (along with palm kernels and melon seeds, they are the major source of cooking oil). Agricultural products are significant only in relation to the needs of the outside, Western world.

In other areas of their life, the standards of judgment are supposed to be Western. A passage on Ibadan, a city of a few millions in western Nigeria, draws unnecessary comparisons between the city and Western cities:

> You do not see the neat arrangement of broad streets that are
> typical of modern European and American cities. (EE 2: 157)

Other African cities do not escape a similar fate: "...When Gaberones becomes the London of Bechuanaland Lobatsi will be its Manchester..."(EE 3: 29). It is not clear precisely how this is supposed to help students understand what their cities look like. All it can do is set the West up as the absolute standard of judging the students' world. With frequent exposure to such comments, it is no surprise that students are often later heard judging their political, economic, and social systems by Western standards. And, like the PE series, most of the non-African passages are Western.

Several of the composition assignments also suffer from shortcomings similar to those in the PE series. Students write about visits to a farm, but they never write about their own farming experience (even though a large percentage are children of farmers), and they go to such places where "shop assistants" ask them: "Do you want self-tapping screws, Sir? [or] Do you want a single-reflex camera?" (EE 1: 112). This is preposterous, to say the least. Once again, we are back on the streets of London or New York.

In EE 3, suggested points for an essay on "Why people should give financial support to their immediate family" draws exclusively upon Biblical and Koranic injunctions:

> The Bible says 'It is more blessed to give than to receive'...
> A Muslim is required by his religion to give alms to the poor...(280)

Are the students' indigenous religions not important as sources of inspiration to do good deeds? Yet another non-indigenous cultural concept is introduced and validated in EE 4. In a passage on letter writing, the student is supposed to say:

> There's one thing I want to escape from at home. You know
> my six-month-old brother--he's all right, of course, but when Mum
> and Dad go out in the evening I have to stay at home and 'babysit'
> for them. Spoils my evenings rather". (113)

Were the subliminal cultural message not so important this excerpt would make for great comedy. The concept of 'baby-sitting' is not African. Even among the elite few, a child looking after his or her younger siblings is not likely to complain that he's being asked to 'babysit'. Looking after your younger sibling is not a choice, but a duty which you grow up to expect and fulfill, and I might add, quite often enjoy because it makes you feel grown-up.

There are, however, a few good assignments whose value is diminished because the lack of previous discussion leads to an overcompensation in the form of giving students what they will write:

1.   A letter to the press

Write a letter to a newspaper on one of the topics below. It should be possible for you to use the 'general to the particular' sequence in one or more of your paragraphs.

    1.   European names for African towns, streets or institutions...

    3.   The need for improving some public service (e.g., the postal service, education) (EE 3: 114)

2.   Your Japanese pen-friend, Haruko Otaki, is fascinated by the fact that you use several languages for a variety of different purposes. She is studying English as a foreign language in her last year at school before going on to university. But she only uses English to read her English books and to write to you. She wants you to give her a full account of the purposes for which you use you mother tongue, a creole language, any other language of your country, pidgin or any other language that you make use of. Write to her, giving her this information and making it clear how much or how often you use each language for each purpose...(EE 5: 120)

3.   Write an article on the function of the extended family in a changing society. Your discussion will probably centre around the extent to which members of a family can reasonably be expected to help both close and distant relatives in such matters as educating them, providing them with board and lodging, giving them or finding them employment, etc. ...(EE 5: 167)

One final comment about the composition assignments in both the PE and the EE series. Students are busy writing to their pen-friends, talking about 'what happened in class yesterday', and analyzing their community for the benefit of their "overseas" pen-friend, or some magazine, alone. They are never working with others on any problem. Ohmann (1976), writing about college English textbooks, describes the situation accurately:

> ...the student is almost invariably conceived of as an individual. He acts not only outside of time and history, but alone--framing ideas, discovering and expressing himself, trying to persuade others, but never working with others to make a theme that advances a common purpose...(149)

Such presentation styles cannot but encourage a destructive brand of individualism in students; it also presents to them a false view of reality--one in which they act alone.

I would like to make some further pertinent general comments on the other sections in these textbooks. Students will find many of the examples in the PE series--particularly the first three books--alienating because they either are conceptually foreign, or encourage an uncritical acceptance of non-indigenous sociocultural attitudes. Many of these examples use too many foreign names in explaining grammatical structures:

> John: Where are you going?
>
> Mary: Down to the market.
>
> John: What do you want to buy?
>
> Mary: A new pen for Joseph. (PE 1: 7)

We confront Tom, Mary, John, Joseph, David, etc., on virtually every page illustrating grammatical structures in this and other books. One may wonder whether, even though they are in an English language class, students do need to be drowned in an avalanche of English names to learn to use English in their, or for that matter, any other community.

At other times, it is not only the names but the sites and landmarks that are alien:

> John: I've seen Westminster Abbey.
>
> Mary: Oh! Have you been to London, then?
>
> Joseph: Yes, John's been all over Europe.
>
> Mary: When did you go, John?
>
> John: My father took me when I was twelve. (PE 1, 68)

Sometimes, a subtle redefinition of the patterns of social relationships takes place through naming. Such an example if found in the following word-study note from PE 2:

> *family* Note the use of *family*. Mr. Okafor had to maintain a family
> of five--i.e. himself, his wife, and three children. Of course, here in
> Africa, *family* is often used to include nieces, nephews, cousins, etc.
> as well. (3)

The very fact that the information on the African family is parenthetical shows that the thrust of the definition of family here is the Western nuclear family. This is nothing but a denial, or denigration, of students' culture. As the text itself suggests, the extended family is still very strong, and students will feel the need to use *family* in this sense. That the word *family* is not ordinarily used in the same inclusive sense among native speakers (a suggestion which in fact oversimplifies English usage), should not prevent students from thus using and adapting the English language to their own needs. Students should not have to redefine interpersonal relationships simply because of the need to express themselves in a foreign language.

Similarly, the terms "cousin," "niece," and "uncle" are inaccurately used to refer to family relationships. In many of the students' mother tongues, those referred to as uncle or cousin in English would be called father and brother, or sister, respectively because of the "extended family" system. And the way we name relationships obviously usually affects our perception of them. Certainly, our behavior towards someone we call brother, regardless of whether or not he is of the same parentage, can normally be expected to be warmer than toward a cousin. References to husband and wife are also generally in terms of monogamous marital relationships, an experience which would not hold true for a sizable number of the students. The Western, monogamous institution thus becomes the norm, and the voluntary polygamous option of the students' cultures deviant behavior. I will elaborate on this point in my discussion of language ideologies in Chapter Six.

The following conversation piece between the ubiquitous John and Mary from PE 1 provides us with one final example of this phenomenon:

John: When are you going to the market?

Mary: After I've finished my housework.

John: Will you go and see Joseph?

Mary: If I have time.

John: Will you have dinner with him?

Mary: Not unless he invites me.

John: Why don't you ask him?

Mary: Because he might not want me to stay. (25)

Perhaps a handful of members of the elite class "invite" friends to dinner. Except on festive occasions, you do not formally invite people to come and dine with you; if friends pay you a visit and find you at dinner, you invite them to join you, and they do so, if they wish. What is going on here is the unwitting acculturation of students to Western modes of behavior. Many students may easily grow up believing that this is the way a "civilized" person ought to behave and, therefore, abandon the warm and informal relationship which traditionally has governed behavior among friends.

If examples like those above continue to abound in textbooks then the process of developing literacy in English cannot but continue to be largely one of alienation. It translates into an experience which cannot equip learners with the ability to take their place in the continuation of their people's culture-making process. Besides what amounts to political illiteracy on the part of authors, some of these problems are traceable to a desire to sell across different countries. It is however possible even with minimal effort to find material suitable for the relevant African countries, given the similarities of culture and colonial experience. And the preponderance of Nigerian material would in fact indicate that Nigeria remains the primary market.

C. Conclusion

The reading passages and essay themes in these books would suggest a conservative educational, economic, and political philosophy. This is the most charitable understanding one can have of the intention of the authors. Since the primary aim of the texts is to teach grammar and "correct writing" and to prepare students for examinations, the development of a critical sociocultural and political awareness is, apparently, not considered important. Material of relevance to students' reality is in fact included only as a means to an end.

It is important to note that when the chips are down, the students are just being groomed for the West African School Certificate Examination (WASCE), to meet the certification requirement at the end of the high school years. Certification at this stage either initiates the students into the modern sector of the economy, or into the third stage of the system, the university. The success or failure of the teacher, indeed the school as a whole, is measured in terms of the percentage of students that succeed in this international certification examination. Therefore, the general assumption seems to be that if what it takes to make students reach this goal is to feed them with 'facts' on the part of teachers, and memorization of everything the teacher or the textbook says, then so be it. The fact that education is also a process of socialization is lost.

All in all, the teaching of English today has changed little from the colonial times. This is not surprising since the goals of education in general have themselves changed little. As Fafunwa (1974) correctly notes,

> By and large, the present goals of Nigerian secondary schools are similar to the goals of secondary education in colonial times. Indeed, except for a few minor modifications, the structure, content, and teaching methods of secondary schools in Nigeria follow closely those of Britain, in spite of the cultural, political and economic differences which exist between the two countries. (193)

It is obvious then that the relationship between the educational system and the polity, a relationship which political philosophers since Plato and Aristotle have argued (that the school system is a reflection of the state), has largely escaped those involved in language education. In Nigeria, like much of the "Third World," educational planners have continued to view education largely in a traditional, utilitarian role of serving objectively identifiable societal needs such as economic development. In this regard, Coleman (1965) correctly states what happens in several developing countries:

> The few pioneering studies of education...have concentrated mainly on manpower needs and the array of skills essential for economic and industrial development. The relationship of education to political development has been almost entirely neglected, although the folklore contains many ambiguous sentiments about the positive and disruptive effects of the diffusion of education. (v)

Inherent in any educational system is an ideology. Regardless of the many functions such as, for example, the political, economic, social selection, that education may be intended to perform, we may see the fundamental goal as, in the words of Althuser, the institutionalization of a particular "cultural hegemony". In the context of the Nigerian educational system, the goals of instruction in English language are to equip learners with the ability to communicate in Nigeria's multilingual setting; to be able to understand and express their knowledge in other subjects; and to be able to communicate in international settings as appropriate. In the light of the analysis of the textbooks and school situation here, however, language education only seems to facilitate the institutionalization of a Western "cultural hegemony" initiated in the colonial period.

In the view of the colonizers and, unfortunately but predictably, not a few Nigerians, culture belonged only to the colonizers. Their peoples' history was presumed to have begun with the "civilizing" presence of the colonizers at that time. And today, culture is often equated with a celebration of the values and artifacts of the peoples' past, including those which clearly are anachronisms. Such understanding of culture as simply customs, a "degenerate culture," is limited and static. Hence, it is erroneous. Culture must be seen largely in terms of the dynamic present, a view Fanon (1967) asserts when he writes of the Vietnamese resistance to the French occupation. He believes that those Vitnamese who willingly gave up their lives in defense of their country did so not for the sake of recapturing some mythical past. Rather, they did so for the sake of a present and a future for their children, a future which would be determined by thier own society.

The thrust of the argumentation here is not that the presence or absence of one kind of material or the other will be held responsible for the social and political consciousness that students eventually develop. It is not even that there should be no foreign material in the books. It is a question of balance and treatment. When authors adopt a cavalier attitude to the significance of textbook material for the questions of power and ideology, they are liable to reinforce the incalculable damage already being done by other forces to the emerging national psyche.

Neither educational institutions, the policies which inform them, nor their curriculum can be neutral given their link to the economy and the relevant dominant social values of the community. Nigeria, like other previously colonized "Third World" countries, it seems reasonable to assume, need to adopt an educational system which is informed by a revolutionary philosophy. Taken in the revolutionary perspective, education is not an ideal, or just a pragmatic solution to a social problem; it should be an important, fundamental political principle, much along the same lines enunciated by the Tanzanian political leadership earlier cited. Writing on post-independence Mozambique, Mugomba has stated this point precisely: "...education for us is the principal instrument for our liberation, for our real political, economic, social and cultural independence" (1980: 216).

In the English language classroom such education translates into something more than increasing the amount of "local material" in textbooks. It is not even a question of say, understanding the history, politics, economy or geography of Nigeria--or any other African country--without reference to Europe or North America, but rather an apprehension of the role of human beings as the principal agents of change in their environment, who have the ability to transform their society's natural resources (human and other), into the material base for a prosperous, sufficiently self-reliant society.

The adoption of this dialectical view of education itself is a necessary precondition to the determination of what would constitute an appropriate language education for previously colonized African societies. Language education will be rooted in an education that either functions as an instrument to be used to facilitate the integration of the younger generation into the logic of the present system, and to bring about conformity to it, or it becomes, in the words of Paulo Freire, "the practice of freedom," the means by which Africans deal critically and creatively with their existential reality, discovering how to participate in their world.

If Africans must include a previous language of colonial domination in their national speech repertoires, then it stands to reason that they should adopt a radical view of its pedagogy, one rooted in an educational system that has chosen the second of our dialectical oppositions. Whatever the characteristics of such a revised pedagogy may be, it must be informed by an educational systems whose central objectives include the following:

    1. the redesigning and operationalization of the educational model--in such a way as to emphasize a new identity and personality (individual/national) purged of colonial imagery, values and aspirations.

    2. the employment of education as an instrument of decolonizing the inherited institutions of Africa's political economy.

    3. making education to contribute directly and positively to the total development (i.e. the political, economic, cultural, and spiritual) of the

society.

The English language curriculum and pedagogy--and indeed that of any other school subject in independent Africa--must take its mandate from these set objectives. In turn, the central objectives of such a situated curriculum and pedagogy of a European language will be:

1. To provide a theoretical framework for teaching students to be functionally literate in the relevant European language as a second language, while simultaneously increasing their critical consciousness, the ability to perceive their socioeconomic and political reality, consequent upon which a stance of critical intervention in created in them. Students must achieve a positive political consciousness, and come to understand education as a humanizing process;

2. To develop a pedagogy of relevance to students' cultural background in order to prevent literacy in the European language from continuing to function as an alienating experience. There must be a development of cultural awareness and the decolonizing of consciousness; literacy pedagogy must become socially integrative. (See Goke-Pariola 1984, 1985 for a fuller articulation of this point of view).

3. To specify teaching methods and materials that will ensure a correlation between the learning of the European language in the students' daily life and the positive aspirations of their society.

Only such steps can mitigate the tragedy of using an alien and previous language of colonial domination as an official language in the African context. It may then become a positive instrument of power. Nobody articulates the rationale for, and the urgency of embracing, these imperatives better than Paulo Freire when he states that:

To acquire literacy is more than to psychologically and mechanically dominate reading and writing techniques. It is to dominate these techniques in terms of consciousness; to understand what one reads and to write what one understands; it is to communicate graphically. Acquiring literacy does not involve memorizing sentences, words, or syllables--lifeless objects unconnected to an existential universe--but rather an attitude of creation and recreation, a self-transformation producing a stance of intervention in one's context. (1980: 48)

Africans need to shatter the myth of the neutrality of the educational process, learn to consciously appreciate its political and ideological character, and take consequent action to realign power in favor of their own cultures.

CHAPTER FIVE

SYMBOLIC POWER AND LANGUAGE USE IN PUBLIC AND PRIVATE SPACE

A. Introduction

Language policy is one thing; the reality of the market place is quite another. In this chapter, I will continue the discussion of the language situation begun in the preceding chapter by asking the question, *How is the struggle for power and the legitimation of particular cultural ideologies carried on outside the school system?* I will discuss the practice of language use in various domains outside the school, such as public administration, the media, religion, popular culture, and inter-personal communication, in the context of both of explicit and implicit language policies and group agenda, as well as the operation of non-explicit sanctions. In other words, the discussion will focus on how the practice may converge with, or diverge from, government policy, how well the school has socialized students into the preferred linguistic ideology, and the complex pattern of factors which determine individual decisions on language choice and language use, as well as the implications of all this for the power differentials between English, and other previous--and in some situations still current--languages of colonial domination and indigenous languages.

B. Public Administration

As the official language of the country, English is the major, if not the exclusive, language of administration in Nigeria. At the federal level, all government business is conducted in English; memoranda, government regulations, and minutes of meetings are written in no other language but English. All courts in the federal judicial structure also conduct their business in English. Needless to say, the laws themselves are written in English. In this regard, the fate of the Nigerian who is not literate in English is no better than that of his counterpart in colonial days. He loses all power to defend himself, and has to be entirely at the mercy of the lawyer and the court interpreter.

While English predominates in state administration, other languages also feature now and then. In the short-lived existence of the Second Republic (1979-1983) for example, of the then nineteen state legislatures, four selected Yoruba, two Igbo, and seven Hausa--all in addition to English. Six also chose English exclusively (Akinnaso 1989). For some state legislatures that chose to carry on the House business in Hausa in addition to English, it was as much a nationalistic act as well as a pragmatic one. Several of the legislators in the northern states simply were unable to communicate in English. In fact, it has been alleged that not a few of the representatives of northern states in the national legislature were in the same predicament. One, in particular--the object of cartoons in national dailies--was alleged to have taken the prudent decision to sleep through the Senate proceedings, only to be woken up when it was time to cast his vote. Unfortunately, such an obviously expressed need for linguistic accommodation did not move the national legislature to implement the constitutional provisions for the use of the three major languages in the national assembly.

Whatever the reasons behind each state's choice, the patterns are clear. First, the linguistic genocide implied in both the *National Policy on Education* (*NPE*) and the *Constitution* seem to have been enforced here. Only the three major languages have at least been honored with the status of co-official languages of legislation. On the basis of their constitutional privileges they not only had the political clout to brow-beat whatever linguistic minorities might exist in some of these states, but the linguistic fragmentation of some of the so-called minority states in the Southeast and the Middle-Belt has not helped matters either.

Astute politicians are, of course, very careful in the way they use their precious legitimate competence--English. While most states continued the business of administration and legislation in English, several high ranking government officials regularly delivered public addresses in indigenous languages. Obviously, the fact that speech is generally less formal than writing played a part in the decision to do so. Public addresses were more often than not political speeches. In which case, since a majority of the target audience did not speak English, speaking the local language was a way to identify with them. Like the Béarnaise mayor of Pau whom Bourdieu cites as having addressed his Béarnaise audience in Béarnaise, a "dialect," rather than the expected legitimate language, Parisian, (and to great applause), Nigerian politicians also often employ the strategies of condescension (Scotton's "downward accommodation"). The governor of Oyo State, Bola Ige, for example, delivered his inaugural address in Yoruba, besides English. This strategy enabled him to derive profit by upsetting the supposed hierarchical relationship between the languages in the national speech repertoire. Using the common touch where one is expected to use the formal speech variety enables one to combine the profits associated with undiminished hierarchy with those derived from what clearly constitutes a symbolic negation of the established linguistic hierarchy. For others, such as Kenya's Arap Moi who uses Swahili, however, it may sometimes be a case also of the lack of real ability in the preferred competence, English.

Since the Second Republic fell victim to a military coup in December 1983, what might have become a linguistic trend has been aborted. The common spectacle is to see high-ranking government officials addressing local communities in English, a language they do not speak. The military, in any case, does not claim to derive its legitimacy from the ballot; rather, the gun is the great legitimizer. So, unlike politicians, they do not often feel the need to play the political game of solidarity. There is in fact often a feeling that the military feels compelled to demonstrate the absolute nature of its power. Speaking a language that emphasizes oneness with the people is not a sign of power; rather, English, the language of the former masters--and now that of the elite--is the language of distance and power, as opposed to the local languages which are languages of solidarity. Their public use is now largely restricted to low-level officials, such as agricultural extension officers, cooperative agencies officials and the like who need to deal with a predominantly non-English-speaking rural clientele. In this case, it would be self-defeating to use any language other than the local one.

Although the federal government distributes some public enlightenment information in the three major languages, at the state level the use of local languages for public information is much more systematic and extensive. Here, several of the minority languages are regularly used in posters dealing with public outreach programs.

The variety in the court systems at the local level also has allowed the use of more local languages. In magistrate (municipal) and customary law courts, for example, the local languages are regularly used. The records are, however, usually kept in English. Also, even though this implies some measure of accommodation for the non-Western educated, it is also a signal of lower class status. To go to a traditional court is a sign of one's low status. Certainly, no member of the elite class would voluntarily go to a customary court. These proceedings of these courts are in fact constant butts of jokes among the Westernized elite. Further evidence is that marriages conducted according to customary law are looked down upon as well. So, there are power implications even in the choice of courts. Also, in the Muslim north where there are *sharia* courts, Arabic is regularly used alongside other local languages.

Tanzania offers a strikingly different example from the Nigerian situation. Here, Swahili, an African language, arguably occupies the position of a preferred legitimate competence. Some of the historical circumstances which gave rise to this possibility have already been discussed. With no single ethnic group dominating political life, and with religious identifications which do not even begin to coincide with ethnic differences (26% Christian, 25% Muslim, and the rest traditional) (Jean O'Barr 1976) and an African socialist philosophy, it has been relatively easy to pursue most public discourse and business in an African language without a loss of power. The story has, however, not been an unequivocal success.

William O'Barr (1976) points out a most interesting use of language to regain what is perceived as loss of local initiative in the socialist system as practiced in Tanzania. This takes place in the Pare Highlands, about 100 miles from the Indian Ocean coast. Here, Swahili is the language of education, government, religion, and politics (meetings of TANU). The local language, Pare, is reserved for the home and local economic activities such as farming and herding. O'Barr reports a series of incidents involving a request by party officials that the Pare people do community work to widen the local roads. Naturally, the local population had not been consulted before this decision was taken. To add insult to injury, they do not own cars that would travel the roads; the party official, who are not locals, will be the principal beneficiaries. Therefore, at meetings with party officials to discuss these projects, the locals, who had to speak Swahili, employed the use of a local marking style called *kingua* ("double talk") to conceal their meaning. As an example of how *kingua* operates, O'Barr cites a hypothetical conversation whose phonological and syntactic features do not differ from ordinary, everyday speech:

1. Where is *Mapombe?*
2. He is with a friend, but the elder *Nzano* is looking for him. If *Nzano* meets up with him, he'll call *Mapombe* away.

Overtly, this conversation appear to be about two men, Mapombe and Nzano. But to understand another meaning which it may have, we must consider the system of naming in this community. In addition to family names derived from kinsmen in one's grandparent's generation, a Pare child is typically given another name which refers to an event surrounding the child's birth. Such a name might be *Sensia* ('on the path', perhaps referring to the fact that the child was born on a path) or *Navwasi* ('illness', perhaps referring to the child's or the mother's bad health at the time of the birth). In the verbal exchange above, the conversation could refer to the natural events which these personal names also represent. The personal name *Mapombe* means 'water'. while *Nzano* is 'sunshine'. Thus, the conversation instead might be understood as follows:

1. Where is the *water?*
2. It's with a friend [in this case, the earth or the fields], but when the sun catches up with it, it will take the *water* away.

A person overhearing this exchange may not comprehend its real meaning, for even this simple example contains much room for manipulation. One possibility is that the speakers really wish to talk about the two men instead of water and sunshine. In such case, the speakers might elaborate their discussion of the rain, the dampness of the field, the weather, etc. On the other hand, attempting to communicate covertly about the elements of nature, for whatever reasons they might have, they could carry on a protacted [*sic*], carefully fabricated, but overtly false exchange about certain people using their names given to describe the birth events or perhaps, to conceal their real intentions even further, using any of the other names which people are called. (1976: 124-5)

In the specific example of the VDC meetings with TANU officials, while to uninitiated Swahili-speaking participants (such as the party officials were) the locals seemed to be spelling out elaborate plans for the community projects, including specific dates, and who would do what, they were in effect communicating to each other the message that noone would participate. Party officials always left feeling they had accomplished their mission. Only, no roads were expanded (O'Barr 1976: 122-132). Thus, even in a situation which seems to be egalitarian in power structure, those who perceive themselves to be outside the power loop have found ways to use language to sabotage the power group.

C. Mass Communication

Both the electronic and print media give us clues as to the relative power of the .different language types in Nigeria. And, once again, the picture changes somewhat as we move from the national to the state or local scenes. First, I will address the electronic media.

Both the language use and the effects of the electronic media are significantly influenced by the fact that the state controls all radio and television broadcasting. (Early in 1993 the government however approved the establishment of privately-owned television and radio stations). Naturally, the radio is perhaps more important, given its ability to reach every nook and corner of the country, in contrast to the television whose influence is limited both by the cost of receiving sets as well as the power of transmitting stations. Here, the government exercises influence via the national broadcasting service, the Federal Radio Corporation of Nigeria (FRCN) (formerly National Broadcasting Corporation--NBC). The government seeks to promote national integration by its use of this medium, or more properly, to impose the dominant ideology of whatever government is in power. This is supported by the fact that until sometime in the late 70s, any state-owned radio station could broadcast on the Medium Wave as well as the Short Wave, the latter allowing them to reach beyond the immediate boundaries of their state/region, and even to broadcast outside the country. In order to limit the potential for the use of these media either to controvert the official line, or for mischief, the federal government prohibited all stations beside the federal one from transmitting on Short Wave. Until then, regional radio stations broadcasting in Hausa, Igbo and Yoruba, could have reached their kin in all parts of the country. Since they often broadcast extensively in the relevant local language they had the potential to reach their kin in a language that they understood. Therefore, by limiting the radio waves, the government was also limiting language choice and use.

Until 1979, the Federal Radio Corporation of Nigeria (FRCN) broadcast national programs in Hausa, Yoruba and Igbo. Now, all its programs at the national level are in English only. However, there are four zonal centers, three of which run programs in local languages:

Northern (Kaduna) Zone: English, Hausa, Fulfude, etc.

Western (Ibadan) Zone: English, Yoruba, Edo, etc.

Eastern (Enugu) Zone: English, Igbo, Efik, etc.

Lagos (National) Zone: English only.

The reason that national broadcasts in indigenous languages by the national zone were stopped is indeed quite revealing of the potential problems with the government's language policies. In a personal interview in 1989, the Director of Programs at the FRCN in Ikoyi, Lagos, said that the broadcasts had to stop because minority language groups incessantly complained that they suffered linguistic discrimination since their languages were excluded from use. We should bear in mind that this reaction was in spite of the fact that the FRCN had originally broadcast in more than the three major languages (In addition to Hausa, Yoruba, and Igbo, the following languages were also used following the creation of more states in the late 70s: Kanuri, Tiv, Efik, Fulfude, and Ishan (Ijaw)). The implication is that even broadening membership of the select group of privileged "national" or "quasi-official" languages is not sufficient to stem feelings of linguistic prejudice on the part of the substantial number of ethno-linguistic communities so excluded. The solution effected at the federal level was ingenuous: shift the blame unto local zones. As part of its program to promote the three major languages, the "network" news is also broadcast at least twice daily in Hausa, Igbo and Yoruba, besides English. Similarly, major national policy broadcasts by the President and federal ministers are normally translated into these three languages.

The language policies of state governments, each of which owns at least a · Medium Wave radio station (some also have FM stations), are dictated both by the need to control information, the need to mobilize citizens and to promote broad-based community awareness, as well as pragmatism. Thus, programs are broadcast not only in a variety of local languages, but even in the dialects of some. Music, drama, storytelling, festivals, rituals, public service announcements, and advertisements are all broadcast in local languages besides English. The latter is a pragmatic move: Since vast numbers of the population are still illiterate in English, for public service announcements and advertisements to be maximally effective they simply have to be delivered in local languages, besides in English.

Having said this, it should be noted that English still largely remains the preeminent medium of communication over the radio. Clearly, at the federal level it is. At state levels, FM stations have almost upstaged the Medium Wave Stations not only in urban areas where they are virtually the only stations patronized, but in several other rural or semi-rural communities. The attraction, as elsewhere, is the music, with fewer interruptions by news and other programs. Even more than perhaps in a place like the United States of America, since the stations are publicly owned the advertisements are comparatively fewer. By and large, much of the music is pop, reggae and rhythm and blues. Even a lot of songs by local artists are also rendered in English. The reasons for this and the implications for the power of English relative to the indigenous languages will be discussed under popular culture in this chapter.

With television broadcasts the picture is quite similar. The National Television Authority (NTA) is divided into zones similar to the FRCN's. Two major differences exist, however. First, virtually all programs at the National (Lagos) Zone are in English. Perhaps given the non-availability of cable services until recently (a few cities such as Lagos and Ibadan have privately owned cable services which enable subscribers to receive international television stations like CNN via satellite) and the limited range of television stations, the trend has been to establish NTA stations in each state of the Federation. As of 1989, there were at least 17 local NTA stations, and at least 12 state-owned stations. The responsibility for delivering translations of major broadcasts often falls on the local NTA stations. Still, most of their programs are run in English. An analysis of a sample program (*NTA Ibadan, Third Quarter Programme Schedule (June 25 - September 23) 1989*) in fact demonstrates this clearly. Of the approximately 58 hours of transmission in the week, English is used for 43 hours, or about 75% of the time, while the total air time in Yoruba, the local language, is 15 hours, or approximately 25% of air time. The gap between Yoruba and English is even more glaring when we look at the picture for weekend transmission which is when the largest viewership is recorded. On Saturdays and Sundays only, the station broadcasts from 12.00 p.m. till about 11.30 p.m. (On weekdays, the station begins transmission at 4.30 p.m.), that is, a total of about 23 hours for both days. English programs occupy 18 hours of weekend air time, that is, about 79% of weekend air time, while Yoruba programs are allotted a total of 5 hours, or 21%. I believe the picture speaks for itself. Yet, this is not only the oldest and most-experienced television station in the country, it is, as its station call and program schedule always proudly announce, "Africa's First Television Station". (The first television station to be established in Africa, it began operating as the Western Nigeria Television Service (WNTV) in 1960 and was taken over by the federal government in the mid 70s and renamed NTA).

State-owned television stations operate much like their radio counterparts. However, English is used more often on these stations than on the radio. A large percentage of the audience for the television programs is concentrated in the urban centers and smaller towns where, to begin with, there is electrical power. These are also the areas where people have both the money to purchase television sets and the time in the evenings to sit down and watch the programs. Obviously, a farmer who has done back-breaking work from sun-up till sundown is less likely to be able to sit down to watch television even if he were fortunate enough to own a television set and to live in a home with electricity.

We can only conclude that the power of English in both radio and television broadcasting remains far greater than the number of its effective speakers would suggest. Even more important, the power of television today is no less than it is in the industrialized countries of the world such as the U. S. A. And if English is the dominant medium of this industry, then we can only imagine what that means to the formation of the consciousness of the viewership, a sizable percentage of which is young. This is the language that conditions how the middle class constructs its identity. The hegemony of English is often by omission on the part of government and industry. For example, when an excellent Yoruba drama series, "*Arelu*", ran on the Ondo State Television Service (OSTV), large numbers of people, including the educated elite, hurried home to watch the weekly episodes. Also, the Wednesday evening Pidgin English television series "*Basi*" by Ken Saro-Wiwa has an estimated viewing audience of 30 million, while an earlier series, equally in Pidgin English, "*Masquerades*," was also very popular. I will return to the implications of this pattern of language use in my discussion of popular culture and the power differential between indigenous and foreign cultures later in this chapter.

Finally, a few comments about the print media. It is estimated that, as of 1989, there were 18 daily and 30 weekly newspapers in Nigeria. According to Paxton (1989) "the aggregate circulation is about 1 million, of which the *Daily Times* (Lagos) has about 400,000". He also cites four more dailies published in Lagos, four in Ikeja, three in Enugu, and four in Ibadan. As Oyelaran (1991) correctly observes, the number of newspapers is not only grossly underestimated, it also seems to include English-only newspapers. There are at least three weekly newspapers in Yoruba--*Isokan* (Concord Publications), *GbounGboun* (Sketch Publishing Company), and *Irohin Yoruba* (African Newspapers (Tribune) Publishing Company). Concord Publications also publishes newspapers in at least two other languages, Hausa and Igbo. Several State Governments similarly publish newspapers not only in English but in some other predominant local language. And with the creation of 10 new states in October 1991 as well as the changeover to a civilian government in 1992 at the state level, we can only expect the number of newspapers to increase as political parties and organizations strive to peddle influence.

Whatever their numbers may be, there is no doubt that the predominant language of newspapers is English. The importance of English is not only quantitative but, perhaps more importantly, qualitative. The major opinion makers, *The Guardian*, *The Daily Times*, *The Punch*, *The New Nigerian*, *The Sketch*, and *The Tribune* are all written in English. Perhaps the new flagship, *The Guardian*, is respected not only for the quality of its reports, but more importantly, for the high standard of English usage. The major weekly newsmagazines, *Newswatch*, *The*

African Guardian, and *African Concord* are all published in English and are modeled after the American newsmagazines, *Time* and *Newsweek*. The significance of this choice of language for the evolution of the consciousness of the middle class, and by cultural osmosis the lower class, will also be discussed under popular culture later in this chapter.

Until the recently announced change in government policy it was only in the print media that private ownership was allowed by law. While there are still no private radio or television stations, several newspapers written in English and local languages and, in fact, all the newsmagazine mentioned above are privately owned. That these news media have also chosen to operate primarily in English is both a pragmatic recognition of the social, economic and political realities of Nigerian society as well as a consequence of educational policies begun by colonial administrations and continued by subsequent post-independence governments. The chickens have indeed come home to roost.

The Republic of South Africa offers an interesting example of a reversal of patterns of language use in response to changing political circumstances. While there is little reported change in the pattern of language use at home, there are the very beginnings of a shift--at least in the repertoire inventory--in public space. The 1991 census reveals that for 95% of the Asian population, English is the home language, while 39% of white, 15% of Coloureds and 0.2% of blacks use English. 65% of whites and 83% of Coloureds used Afrikaans. As for African languages, Zulu leads as home language (38.7%), followed by Northern Sotho (15.1%) and Xhosa (12.7%). Obviously, for whites and Coloureds, and indeed blacks too, the span orientation in public space is towards English an Afrikaans. However, in a dynamic response to the probability of "a new [black-dominated] South Africa", some white professionals are beginning to add African languages to their repertoire. Journalists seem to be in the vanguard of this movement. For example, as reported by the daily *The Cape Times*, 18 of its staff members have enrolled in a Xhosa course (March 13, 1992). The article by Nohmle ("a.k.a. Fiona Chisolm"), concludes that "The greatest bonus for all the hard work [involved in learning the new language] is to see how even a basic knowledge of Xhosa opens doors to friendship, understanding and communication.... what the new South Africa is supposed to be all about[?]" (8). Of course, it's more than a simple question of "understanding"; people are also beginning to hedge their bets. This fact comes across clearly in Fred Bridgland's article, appropriately titled "More than a language learning experience...," which appeared in the October 21 1991 edition of *The Star*. After observing that there has been "an explosion of adult education classes in northern Johannesburg for domestic workers and other black people wanting to improve their English," he adds that there has equally been a parallel growth "in the number of whites, mainly women, wanting to learn *isiZulu*, *seSotho*, *seTswana*, *sePedi* and *isiXhosa*" (9). People, in particular members of the currently dominant group, are trying to increase their linguistic capital with an eye on "the future South Africa". As Bridgland correctly notes, "In the future South Africa, the ability to speak a black language will be a considerable advantage" (1991: 9).

D. Religion

When we think of language and religion in Nigeria, the connection that perhaps comes to most people's minds is that between Arabic and Islam. Arabic is clearly the language of Islam. After all, for a long time the Koran was not to be translated into any other language so as to preserve the words of God who supposedly spoke to Mohammed in Arabic. Even though the Koran has since been translated into other languages, Arabic is still seen as the ultimate language of the religion, perhaps because the majority of Muslims are still Arabic speakers. The situation on the ground is however more complex. Of interest here is not what language is used to worship in what religion per se, but rather if there is choice, and what such choice may say about the individual, or class, in relation to power, or ideology.

With Islamic religion the situation is quite simple. Arabic remains the preferred language of worship. Many Muslims already would be able to recite the Koran, which they would have committed to memory in Koranic schools. Of course, at the end of their training, they cannot claim to speak the classical Arabic in which the Koran is written--in fact they have mastered no conversational skills in Arabic; all they can do is either recite, or follow a recitation of the Koran in Arabic. This is however not to deny the fact that some of the leaders do proceed to master the language itself, enough to deliver a Jumat preaching in it. But, even then, the readings from the Koran and any speech delivered in Arabic will be simultaneously translated into the relevant local language by the interpreters. The situation, therefore, is that for virtually all worshippers Arabic is a foreign language, and almost all will need to have the message translated into their own mother tongues. Linguistically then, there is a significant degree of equality in the mosque.

With Christianity, the situation is quite different. Like Islam, Christianity was initially largely associated with a foreign language, English. After all, the English people introduced the religion. In fact, as already noted in Chapter One, this association between the language, people, and religion partially affected the fate of Western education in the Muslim north during the colonial period. Perhaps if Christianity had been introduced into Nigeria before the Reformation, Christianity might have had a Church language, Latin, comparable to Arabic. As it was, even though the Roman Catholic Church maintained Latin as the language of the Church, the Protestant churches initially operated on the basis of using English and the indigenous languages. It must be emphasized that unlike the rationale for the several translations of the Bible into English which culminated in the Authorized Version in 1611, the impetus here was not a recognition of the validity of the Protestant belief that one should read and interpret the Bible for oneself. To do that, it must be assumed that one is capable of reason. As any student of colonial history knows, colonized peoples, particularly black Africans, were not deemed to have been particularly imbued with such quality as reason, since they had remained "primitive savages". The fact of the matter was that in mother tongue literacy Christian missionaries found the cheaper, quicker, and more efficient way to introduce the Bible to Africans. Consequently, they pursued with vigor the alphabetization of several languages and proceeded to sponsor the translation of the Bible into them.

But ever since the first missions were established, a linguistic dichotomy which roughly parallels class lines has developed in much of the Christianized south. As briefly illustrated in Chapter One, the more educated many Christians became the more they sought to be like their European mentors. Speaking English was but one manifestation of this syndrome. What has since happened in most mainstream congregations is that two types of services have developed in most urban centers. The early service in most Anglican (Episcopalian) Churches, for example, is conducted in English and usually lasts about an hour. Later on Sunday mornings, the second service is conducted in the local language and may last up to two hours. It also borrows more from elements of traditional worship. Since the sermon is delivered in the indigenous language, for example, cultural allusions are acceptable for the purpose of illustrating biblical points, while music with African rhythms plays a significant part in the worship. In the rural areas, of course, the services are conducted exclusively in the local language, given the composition of the congregation, many of whom are literate in the local language, but not English.

It is really the linguistic choice of the educated middle class that provides the most interesting observation here. Most members of this group choose to attend the early English service or mass. For some, the explanation is simply that it is shorter and therefore less "boring". For yet a sizable group, they can neither follow the scriptural readings nor the hymns in their mother tongue because they are functionally illiterate in it. Yet many others feel that the service conducted in the mother tongue is for the lower classes. Therefore, the medium of the service one attends says something about one's class, or one's aspirations, since several of these educated people are much poorer than some of their illiterate or semi-literate kin. As a matter of fact, the behavior of some elderly people who attend the local service and pretend to follow the hymns while dancing to the alter (but with the hymn books turned upside-down--a testimony to their illiteracy) is a constant source of comedy among the educated middle class. In several mainstream Christian denominations, then, language is closely related both to individual ideology and group power. It is difficult to imagine anything more intimate than religious practice and thought; yet, for many, English dominates even in these innermost recesses of the soul.

The picture is admittedly more complex than I have presented here. Beginning in the 1890s, the secessionist movement in the Protestant Church of Lagos encouraged the use of indigenous music and dance as means of propagating the gospel. Consequently, several variants of the Protestant faith developed. The more these sects incorporated Yoruba culture into their theology and liturgy, the further they moved away from the "acceptable mainstream" of the Protestant faith. As one moves further away from the mainstream churches, the picture changes dramatically. Good examples of these are the Apostolic Church, the Cherubim and Seraphim Church, and the Celestial Church of Christ. These are churches that have tapped substantially into those aspects of Christianity which seem to fit in with African cosmology. Here, members of the Westernized elite class become linguistic chameleons. These are churches that emphasize the agency and potency of demons, witches, wizards, voodoo, magic, healing, possession, and all other features and beliefs of charismatic churches.

The reasons why these churches are so popular, then, goes very deep into traditional culture. Africans have found the "prefabricated theology" brought into Africa to be inadequate for their needs. They want a theology which bears "the stamp of original thinking and meditation of Africans" (Bolaji-Idowu 1975: xi). As Kofi Appiah-Kubi (1981) discovered in his study of such churches in Ghana as well, they are most popular because they not only recognize but also greatly emphasize the "spiritual experience". These churches not only serve as therapeutic communities, they also emphasize healing. In the latter respect, their strategy compares with traditional healing practices: the use of suggestion, faith in the healer (the prophet), and the healing process.

In the last few years, these churches which were initially considered a fringe phenomenon and the exclusive preserve of the illiterate have now become points of open refuge for members of the elite class seeking protection from the persecution of a modern economy and society. Consequently, exclusive membership in such churches, or simultaneous membership in them and another mainstream church, is no longer considered unusual; rather, it is fast becoming the norm for the elite. Bolaji-Idowu explains the underlying reason for this dramatic development:

> While...every African may wish to be regarded as connected with one or the other of the two 'fashionable' religions, most are at heart still attached to their own indigenous beliefs. It is now becoming clear to the most optimistic of Christian evangelists that the main problem of the church in Africa today is divided loyalties of most of her members between Christianity with its Western categories and practices on one hand, and the traditional religion on the other...in strictly personal matters relating to the passage of life and the crisis of life, African Traditional Religion is regarded as the final succor by most Africans. (1975: 205-6)

What happens then is that these charismatic churches provide a safe middle ground between African Traditional Religion and Christianity.

A direct consequence of the demographic characteristics of their initial clientele as well as the African Traditional Religious foundations of their theology and worship is the choice of indigenous languages in these sects. The African spiritualist church, the Cherubim and Seraphim Church in western Nigeria, for example, conducts its services in Yoruba. The significance of this linguistic choice cannot be overemphasized. Appiah-Kubi writes of these churches:

> ...indigenous African Christian churches...provide a release of
> tension through a cathartic ritual and beliefs that heighten the hope
> of their members. Thus the healing ceremonies of these churches
> involve a union of the patient, his family, the larger group, and the
> supernatural world, by means of a dramatic, emotionally charged,
> esthetically rich ceremony that expresses and reinforces shared
> beliefs. (1981: 81-3)

This goal cannot be successfully carried out except in a language that is a common heritage of the congregation and which reflects the traditions on which the worship is based.

One other reason for the choice of language, of course, is that, traditionally, the church leadership, especially the "prophet-founders," as well as a large percentage of the congregation have not been literate in English. But more importantly--at least in explaining the behavior of the educated middle class who increasingly have patronized these churches--is that the beliefs are more easily expressed in Yoruba. These are faiths that tie into existing cosmological beliefs and religious practices. Much of the evocative power and the charisma, like in sympathetic magic, resides in the power of words. A good example is the Celestial Church whose membership and religious hierarchy is increasingly dominated by the educated middle class and yet retains Yoruba as its language. These churches have also appealed to the middle class and others because, apart from recognizing the active existence of demons and the like, they accept African traditional practices such as polygamy. Many of those who patronize to these churches also have simultaneous membership in the mainstream churches. At public revival meetings, while a Western-style evangelical movement like The Rev. Ben Idahosa's group preaches in English and then translates into a local language, the leaders of these other groups preach in Yoruba and are then translated simultaneously into English. Here, the linguistic and cultural schizophrenia of the Westernized middle class clearly manifests itself. It is really a linguistic and cultural chameleon, its behavior being dictated by its ideological posture at different points, which is ultimately related to questions of power. The implications of this behavior for the identity of the middle class will be discussed in the last chapter.

I have obviously said nothing about the practice of traditional religions. This is for two reasons. First is the nature of traditional religion itself. Second is the group characteristic of the subscribers. Traditional religions constitute more of a way of life and a belief system. They have not generally coalesced into institutionalized set-ups like the evangelical religions. Also, most of the active practitioners--people who operate as priests, diviners, and acolytes who participate in the occasional festivals, are from the poorer, non-Western educated classes. Naturally, the language is local. The middle and upper classes' involvement is ad hoc, based on the need for power. In fact, it may be argued that the simultaneous memberships in the apostolic and spiritualist churches is their way of going "traditional" while remaining "modern," and "Christian". Recently, there has been an attempt to institutionalize one form of traditional religion in the Yoruba-speaking part of Nigeria. In Ibadan, for example, there is a Church of Orunmila (Yoruba Assistant God of Creation), with regular hours of service, and with readings from Ifa (Divination) poetry. There has however been no widespread acceptance of the church.

E. Popular Culture

Popular culture has always been recognized as a veritable battle ground for ideological warfare. Hence the historical attempts to control this form of culture. It has also always been one of the earliest targets of criticism in times of social uncertainty--the one area that points to the impending "destruction of our way of life". Ironically, the supposedly industrialized and freer democracies have often been the most suspicious of popular culture. Anyone familiar with what often passes for serious debate in the United States Congress and media or witnessed the "battle" for the American soul during the 1992 American presidential elections would understand this. Of course, with people like Senator Jesse Helms, such debates will be around for a long time.

The suspicion of the ideological dangers of popular culture is not without foundation however. The world may not come to an end as often predicted. But popular culture serves as a potent, less obviously didactic method of indoctrination into a value system--which partly accounts for its great success all over the world, to the constant dismay of conservatives. It has a way of creeping up both on its acolytes as well as its critics. It also mirrors where society stands and often indicates which way society may be heading. Finally, it gives perhaps the clearest clues as to the ideological orientation and desires of large segments of the population. If culture is described, or defined, as the embodiment of the totality of a people's achievements and aspirations, then the mode of expressing that culture itself symbolizes, or proclaims, the aspirations of those who participate in the culture. It is in this sense that language as a form of popular cultural expression assumes its remarkable significance.

In linguistically monolithic societies which also have a dominant culture, the issue of language as a shaping force of popular culture may not be quite topical. In such situations, language, in all probability, has more do with issues of social stratification or sub-group membership on the basis of wealth, genealogy, or race, for example. However, in several economically and politically underdeveloped "Third World" countries, the vehicle of popular culture becomes important both as a political as well as a cultural statement in the context of international politics.

Until the recent turmoil in the capitalist system, much of Africa, like other "Third World" countries, has been invariably engaged in an uneasy wedlock with the Great Powers--the Soviet Union and the United States of America. Each power claimed to be the protectors of "Third World" countries, either "liberating" them from "capitalist exploitation" or from the "shackles of communism," all depending on which side of the fence you are. Although various strategies have been employed in this process, historical hindsight teaches us that the most effective methods of shackling the political economies of poorer countries to the East or the West seems to have been through control of the mental consciousness of at least a vocal minority of the citizenry of the particular "Third World" country. Once the mentality has been colonized, these locals become the most effective advertisers of the "virtues" of the relevant power. For this kind of economic and political manipulation, the middle class has historically proved fertile breeding ground. In recent times, however, even the lower classes have become highly susceptible. In Nigeria, for example, during the Second Republic the taste bud of the "common man" became so substantially conditioned to Uncle Ben's rice that a scarcity of this "essential commodity" might, in fact, have precipitated a national crisis.

Language has generally been an indispensable factor in empire building (Brosnahan 1965). The case of Nigeria, as previous discussion has shown, was no exception. The overt manipulation of the resources of African and other "Third World" countries in the form of the establishment of economic and political structures favorable to the powers dates back to the beginning of colonialism, with the Berlin Conference of 1844 giving explicit statement to this desire. America joined late in this enterprise because she herself was a colony until late 18th century. Her desire to share in the booty, more than the empty rhetoric about "freedom" and "self-determination," was in fact largely responsible for her interest in the decolonization of Africa, especially after the Second World War.

The termination of formal colonial rule set the stage for the second form of manipulation, neocolonialism, which is simply the non-overt manipulation of the host country's economy. In this stage of colonialism, various institutions such as the World Bank, the International Monetary Fund (IMF), sometimes the United Nations Organization, the Jaycees, the Lions, and sundry other institutions and organizations have aided in the process of economic fostering of "Third World" countries to the West. Perhaps even more important in their role in this venture are the multinational corporations such as the oil companies and Coca-Cola. For example, much of the work of the now defunct English Language Institute (ELI) at the University of Michigan was funded initially by the big American multinational corporations. They were interested in teaching English to Latin Americans as a way of acculturating them to the American way of life and, hence, protecting their huge financial empires and stemming alleged "communist threats" in the region. Other agencies that have also served similar purposes are the British Broadcasting Corporation (BBC) and the Voice of America (VOA).

Popular culture has always served the purposes of covert manipulation of the political economy. In this regard, the vehicular expression of many forms of popular culture gives tremendous advantages to the West and is part of the problem of the crisis of the national political economy in several African countries. I will now briefly comment on the significance of language choice in the following forms of popular culture: popular literature, music, advertising, and fashion.

Until recently, the only viable popular literature available was in the form of what is derisively referred to as "Onitsha market literature". In a period of about twenty years (1947-1966) the tradition produced more than two hundred titles, the most popular of which, *Veronica My Daughter*, by A. Ogali, sold more than 60,000 copies (Obiechina 1972). The books in the "series" had all the characteristics necessary to appeal to a wide and at best semi-literate audience: simplicity of language, brevity of form, and affordability. They also represented perhaps the only major instance when there was an attempt to use English in a manner to include the majority of the people rather than to exclude them from popular literary culture. This contrasts sharply with the elitist characteristics of the Heinemann African Writers Series. Of course, the latter also dealt with more involved and complicated societal themes and could not be considered light reading for most people, well-educated or not.

The vacuum thus created has been readily filled by James Hadley Chase, Harold Robbins, Denise Robins, Jaclyn Susan, Sidney Sheldon, Barbara Cartland, and a host of other writers in the Mills and Boons or Harlequin Romance series. Consequently, the reading public is nurtured on the streets of New York or London, reading about life-styles and world-views markedly alien to their society. For a black person, there must in fact be a masochistic pleasure in reading through much of James Hadley Chase who somehow manages to find dumb, large-nosed, sweaty "niggers". Barbara Cartland, Denise Robins and others write about the "knights in shining armor," the undying romantic loves of Europeans and North Americans. It is no wonder then that the process of alienating the consciousness of the youth in Nigeria is substantially accelerated by such literature. They grow up to judge the social, economic as well as interpersonal spheres of their life by the values implied in the themes of these novels.

In the last two decades, various new forms of popular literature have gained currency amongst Nigerians, from the barely literate to the well-educated. These popular literatures may be in the form of detective/romance stories, comic strips or pornographic literature. The "indigenization syndrome" however appears to have caught up with popular literature. We now have Macmillan's "Pacesetters", Longman's "Drumbeats," and Fagbamigbe's "Eagle Romance". A close examination of the titles and themes of most books in these series however only reveals black masks and white skin. The titles themselves are often quite revealing: *Bloodbath at Lobster Close* (Dickson Ighavini, Macmillan's "Pacesetters"), *The*

Woman Who Won and *Divided Heart*, by Bertha M. Clay, and Rosa Almonte's *Love in the Clouds* (Fagbamigbe's "Eagle Romance"). The closest they get to the society is perhaps no more than the black faces in the cover illustration. In general, they serve as a means of unconsciously engraving the socioeconomic and political values of the West in the psyche of a vocal cross-section of the population.

This non-overt indoctrination into a particular ideology begins for the middle class much earlier in childhood through the comics. They range from the neo-Tarzanic, through *Little Red Riding Hood, Bunty, Whooper,* to *Superman.* Children start out reading these comics for fun, but at the end of the day, aided by an alienating school curriculum that emphasizes Western nursery rhymes with Western folk heroes, the socioeconomic aspirations of the adolescents become embodied in visions of the heroes in these forms of popular literature. It is the children weaned on these comic strips and detective/romance stories that become students in tertiary institutions--"the leaders of tomorrow"--who eventually constitute the indigenous political elite that manage the intellectual and economic life of their society for the benefit of the West and that of their own.

Popular radio and television also contribute to this ideological orphanage. The world services of the BBC and VOA are readily available to the radio listener with the attendant loading with biased Western economic, social and political ideas and values. Even the most discerning and wary listener cannot but sometimes be unconsciously susceptible to the overwhelming cultural invasion inherent in the programs beamed out on these media. Now, with the advent of cable television the choice will be even richer. Perhaps even more potent have been the television and movie theaters. The foreign film industry is dominated by Western movies. Again, the medium--English--makes them most readily accessible to the audience. It is impossible to be exposed to them without in some way yearning for the kind of society that informs them, especially since they are normally portrayed in such glorious terms.

If one may be somewhat tautological, perhaps the most popular form of popular culture is music. And here, once again, the English language plays a significant role. For the youth of today, it is doubtful that the most popular forms of music are indigenous. Among the educated and half-educated, funk and pop music are most popular. The Blacks of the Diaspora have played a significant part in this "backward integration" of colonization. They have made funk and pop very popular. Their music expresses a culture; but even though they are black, the culture is Western. Perhaps the major exception to this would be reggae music which comes from the "Third World" Blacks of the Diaspora. Although there exists a vibrant local popular music culture, the country's linguistic diversity complicates matters. Local musicians who really seek to rise above narrow ethno-linguistic limitations are forced to convey their message in English. They too have been bitten by the love bug of romance. As in other forms of popular culture so far discussed, the English language gives all the advantage to a Western ideology.

Even something as mundane as sign-writing (as in local street-side advertising) gives us a clue as to the influence of language on the sociocultural aspirations of the populace. Streets in the smallest of hamlets are invariably dotted with signposts that advertising the skills of this or that painter, barber, hairdresser, seamstress, etc. Invariably, almost all are *"London"*-or *"New York-trained,"* but never *"Moscow-trained"*. The message is clear: the orientation is, or should be, to the West, from where all good things come.

Finally, one brief look at the world of fashion. Ordinarily, fashion, though recognized as a form of popular culture, does not involve language. But recently, the situation has been changing, especially among the youth. It is a common sight these days to see a young man sporting a T-shirt with the bold inscription, "American Marines," "Carnaby Street," "I Love N.Y.," or the dated hippie line, "Make Love, Not War". And he struts about his neighborhood like a peacock. He need not say anything further about his aspirations: The T-shirt says it all. Wearing a shirt that proclaims him an American marine, or that says he loves New York identifies him psychologically with his aspiration to be Western. This communication between him and the rest of the world is, of course, mediated by the English language.

The major significance of the English language in popular culture lies in its making readily accessible to the populace a Western cultural capital. It lies in the fact that it expresses and conditions the acceptance of, or the longing for, a Western type of political economy. Obviously, at a secondary level of analysis, the use of English contributes to the widening of the power differential between indigenous cultures and Western culture, to the advantage of the West. It reinforces the other forms of invasion--political and economic. It reinforces the lack of communication between the generations. Such communication gap, largely predicated on language choice, makes more difficult the process of cultural transmission, of a continuity of culture, and the realization of the necessary synthesis of indigenous and foreign cultures, since it ceases to be a communal activity. The thrust of the argumentation, as usual, is not cultural insularity, but a conscious effort to revert the power differential in favor of the indigenous cultures and the interest of the generality of the people.

Thus far, the cultural advantage has been to the West. But more importantly, so has the political and economic advantage. This may prove temporary though, because a middle-class that has not organically evolved its own culture based on local cultures cannot provide the kind of climate necessary for a successful Western-type economic and political system which will provide the economic climate and political stability necessary for successful economic penetration by multinational corporations. So far, the end product has been a caricature of the Western bourgeoisie--but one with the most negative characteristics--apathy, resistance to change, materialism, selfishness, and ostentatious consumption.

F. Interpersonal Communication

One final area of language choice and use which requires attention is that of inter-personal communication. How do people as individuals decide on what language to use in different situations? What does this tell us about the relative powers of the several languages, or groups of languages, in the individual's or the nation's speech repertoire?

Unfortunately, in contrast to the case in several other African countries, there is little to guide us by way of empirical research in this area of language use. In her study of African societies, such as that of Kampala, in Uganda, Scotton (1990) identifies the phenomenon of "elite closure". This arises in situations where the preferred language of the elite is distinct from that of the lower groups. She suggests that, in West Africa, the general language that the elite would employ with the excluded masses tends to be Pidgin English, although in Cote d'Ivoire, Dyula pays such a role. In Zaire and the East Coast of Africa, in general, Swahili often fulfills such a function. She concludes that, confronted by such instances of "elite closure," "the great majority of African citizens face linguistic barriers to social mobility" (58). This however seems to be an overstatement of the case. Even the results of her own earlier 1972 study of the use of Swahili in Kampala, Uganda, would seem to call such a conclusion into question. As summarized by Laitin,

> People make individual assessments of the benefits of speaking a language (multiplied by the probability of actually receiving them) and then subtract the cost of learning it. Scotton finds that because Swahili does not reveal ethnic origin or socioeconomic status, it is a useful code for everyday communication where individuals do not want to embroil themselves in status competition. She concludes ... by attributing the considerable use of Swahili to its "good return" to Kampalans who learn and use it. (1992: 32).

Furthermore, one need only consider the ranks of the politically and economic powerful in a country such as Nigeria to find further evidence that contradicts such a blanket assertion.

With respect to Nigeria, the results of a pilot study which I conducted in an urban center in 1987 do however give a clue as to what may be going on, at least in some areas of individual language choice in inter-personal interactions (Goke-Pariola 1987a). The study, which involved questionnaire and personal interviews of about 500 subjects, sought to determine the vehicularity, use and function of Nigerian languages and English, in addition to the attitude of the population to the question of national language. Of the range of factors which may determine or influence language choice, such as setting, participants, purpose, and topic, the questions focused on two--participants and setting--as the primary ones.

The results of the study suggest, among other things, that while in intra-group situations the tendency to use the mother tongue is indeed strong, it is generally overridden by the factors of setting and participants, such as work and role-relationship. A shift in setting from the informal one of home to the formal one of work, just like that from equality to inferiority, entails a shift from the mother tongue into a language of accommodation and distance, English.

In situations where participants do not share a mother tongue, English is the general medium of communication. However, even is this situation, depending on the setting, the addressor's knowledge of the addressee's speech repertoire is taken into consideration: should the addressee possess the addressor's mother tongue in his repertoire, he may be addressed in that language, provided the setting is appropriate. What emerges from this is the fact that language usage and language loyalty or preference are not necessarily co-terminus; more often than not, pragmatism in communication seems to be the rule.

Of particular interest here are the findings of the study in respect of language attitude. In order to determine the respondents' attitude to the various languages or groups of languages in the national repertoire, four questions were asked: Which language do you like best? In which language can you best express yourself? Which language would you like to be the lingua franca? (If all the people in this community could speak the same language, which one would you prefer to use?). Which language would you prefer your children to speak the best?

Over 60 percent of respondents liked their mother tongue best. Even among those who claimed English as their mother tongue, only about 60% said they like it best. These figures clearly demonstrate a healthy and positive attitude to the mother tongue, one likely to encourage their survival in the face of English's apparently relentless onslaught. On the question of the language in which the respondent feels he best expresses himself, that is, the one in which he has the greatest facility, there is an over 10% drop in the number of people who chose their mother tongue. With the exception of Yoruba (60.62%) and Hausa (50%) respondents, less than 50% of the others claim to be able to express themselves best in their mother tongue.

The second and third questions were designed as checks on each other and to determine the respondents' attitude to the national language question. It is interesting in this regard to note the dramatic drop in the number of those who chose their mother tongue in response to either question. While 60.62% chose it in response to the second, only 31.5% did for the third question. Given the fact that the answer to the third question most directly addresses the national language question, we may see and indication of the fate of the three "major languages"-- Hausa, Igbo and Yoruba--along with the other contenders, English and Pidgin, in these figures which show the percentage of respondents that would choose each language:

Hausa:	3.6%	Pidgin:	12.7%
Igbo:	4.8%	Other:	2.6%
Yoruba:	19.4%	Don't Know:	2.6%
English:	54.3%		(N= 495)

Responses to the last question about which language respondents would like their children to speak best varied significantly from that to the question of what language the respondents themselves liked the best. While a vast majority liked their mother tongue best, most would prefer English as the official language. This probably demonstrates a keen sensitivity to the socio-political as well as economic advantages of English as the official language over and above all indigenous languages. Pidgin fails to exercise as much influence as one would have expected in all the responses. The only place it has any significant showing is in respect of the language of business in the market place (Goke-Pariola 1987). This would seem to contradict Laitin's suggestion that Pidgin English, much like other populist urban languages such as Sango in the Central African Republic, Shang and other popular dialects of Swahili in Kenya, Akan-English code switching in Ghana, and popular Lingala in Zaire, might become a significant contender for the national language position in Nigeria's language outcome (1992: 116).

Informal observations of educated Nigerians however shows a less encouraging picture. Even in one of the most intimate activities--letter writing between family members and friends (including love letters)--English is virtually the automatic medium. This is the case even when members all understand the mother tongue. Explanations for this phenomenon are complex. An obvious one is that the art of letter writing was learnt by most in English. But then, several would also have studied their mother tongue formally in school, including the art of letter writing in them. My suspicion is that there is an underlying socio-psychological and pragmatic motivation for their behavior. One explanation is that several people are really illiterate in their mother tongues, regardless of years of schooling in them. It is indeed fashionable to fail in the mother tongue in school, but not in English. In other words, inability to communicate in the mother tongue either in speech or in writing really carries no official or private sanctions for the failing student--it may in fact be considered a badge of honor and a mark of social prestige. Even on university campuses, students who are majoring in indigenous languages are considered social pariahs and are a constant butt of jokes.

Many people also correctly see writing as a formal linguistic act. For such people, even if they were literate in their mother tongue, since English is identified with formality they would still prefer to use English regardless of the fact that the letters are intimate. The only concession they make may be that the language is informal--but, quite often, that is difficult to determine. For anyone who is familiar with Nigerian English would know that, like several other non-native varieties of English, the stylistic variation is minimal, and it tends to remain formal and turgid, reflecting the usually formal mode of its acquisition. Competence in idiomatic English is certainly not one of the strengths of the average writer of English in Nigeria.

Perhaps the most disturbing explanation has to do with the status of English. The use of a local language in inter-personal communication is supposed to be a hallmark of the illiterate, "illiterate" somehow having been interpreted to mean only inability to read and write in English. Several people learned about romantic love from the Western popular fiction they read. Therefore, for them English is the natural language of "love". Others with lower levels of formal education would have schooled themselves for years in the hyperbole and ungrammaticalness of the ever-popular "Onitsha market literature" whose inventory includes copious volumes on the art of love-letter writing.

G. Conclusion

The overall picture one gets from examining language use in both public and private space is that English exhibits a distinctive dominance configuration pattern over all other languages in the nation's as well as the individual's speech repertoire. It is quite clear that even though people may be proud of their mother tongues and sometimes even believe themselves to be most competent in it, they display sufficient sensitivity to the linguistic complexities of the country not to wish to impose their own language on others. In fact individuals show greater common sense and sociolinguistic and political savvy than the government. For pragmatic considerations, English is to be preferred as a lingua franca and, therefore, the language that children need to know best. But they also seem to feel that English is more "sophisticated" and "cultured" language. The realities of the market coupled with government policies also continue to promote English. Thus, the quest for individual and group power propels the status of English while at the same time devaluating indigenous languages.

In what is fast emerging as a diglossic situation, English occupies the H (High) position, and the indigenous languages in L (Low) position. The government however seems bent on splitting the L spectrum in two with the three major languages as higher Ls. What is perhaps most disturbing is the increasing loss of the indigenous mother tongue among the younger generations from Western-educated families. What is happening to the children of several Nigerians living in Europe and North America may provide a clear indication of what will eventually happen in Nigeria, beginning with the urban centers: the displacement of the mother tongues by English.

CHAPTER SIX

SYMBOLIC VIOLENCE AND AFRICAN SOCIOCULTURAL REALITY

A. Introduction

Now, I return to the questions with which the discussion in the present volume began--the relationship between language choice and language use, power (between different classes, socioeconomic groups and the nation and outside powers) and ideology (local cultures versus foreign cultures and world views). My purpose in this chapter, then, is to bring together the various observations which I have made concerning the historical relationship between English and other previous languages of colonial domination and African indigenous languages, and the issue of power and ideology as well as identity. The chapter will seek to illustrate one of the most significant ways in which a language which promotes an ideology which is different from that of the majority culture--or cultures--may facilitate and accelerate a change in the social and cultural reality of a people, particularly if that language is adopted as the medium of intellectual discourse. As an example, the effects of the continued use of English as a primary language by Yoruba peoples of Nigeria on how future generations may come to apprehend their sociocultural reality will be discussed. So will the consequences of language choice for how Africans position themselves, or are positioned, in relation to the industrialized world in the touted "New World Order".

The question has been raised in slightly different, but relevant, contexts. For example, Bretton in a chapter titled "Political Science, Language, and Politics" which is included in the O'Barr and O'Barr volume, *Language and Politics*, asks the question, "If political thought and theory actually influences political behavior, shapes social institutions, and determines social processes, can it be assumed that a language medium suitable for these purposes is available and at work [in modern African states]?" (1976: 437). He answers, "No"--since, as he contends, indigenous languages lack the "technical elaboration to express new ideas". In support of this position, he states as follows:

> If one further considers changes in the mode of production, ongoing incisive demographic changes, and the social and cultural consequences flowing from these, the burdens placed upon indigenous languages in developing countries with respect to the formulation of relevant social thought and theory may prove to be far beyond the present capacity of most of them. This is, of course, as true for economics or religion as it is for politics. (438)

Citing the modified Sapir-Whorf hypothesis--linguistic relativity--he concludes that the communication of political messages across the sorts of linguistic (and thereby cultural) boundaries which exist in most developing countries is precarious indeed. [And that] Ideology, whether generated within the nation or imported from abroad, must pass through many filters indeed, both those which reflect different status positions within any particular country and those which are generated by different language and thought systems. (439)

Besides the fact that Bretton's argument is supported neither by historical evidence nor linguistic fact, the important point which I wish to raise is not whether indigenous African languages have the capacity to carry the weight of Western thought. Rather, it is whether those very thoughts are desirable, and whether the inadvertent or deliberate use of English and other Western languages is not inimical to the sociocultural evolution of African societies as legitimate, distinct entities.

B. Language and Reality

First, the age-old controversy concerning the relationship, if any, between language and ideology, or better, reality and world view. I begin with Fanon's axiomatic statement about the peculiar situation of the colonized. He states that "The colonized is elevated above his jungle status in proportion to his adoption of the mother country's cultural standards". In view of the fact that language is the principal vehicle of culture his conclusion cannot but be pertinent to those "Third World" countries which were formerly European colonies. For as the discussion in preceding chapters has shown, regardless of what fate may have befallen the British empire, "the sun [still] never sets on the English language".

Pierre Bourdieu perhaps best captures the role of language in this construction of social reality when he writes:

> The social sciences deal with pre-named, pre-classified realities which bear proper nouns and common nouns, titles, signs and acronyms. At the risk of unwittingly assuming responsibility for the acts of constitution of whose logic and necessity they are unaware, the social sciences must take as their object of study the social operations of *naming* and the rites of institution through which they are accomplished. But on a deeper level, **they must examine the part played by words in the construction of social reality and the contribution which the struggle over classifications, a dimension of all class struggles, makes to the constitution of classes -- classes defined in terms of age, sex or social position, but also clans, tribes, ethnic groups or nations. ...**
>
> ... [Therefore] social science must include in its theory of the social world a theory of the theory effect which, by helping to impose a more or less authorized way of seeing the social world, helps to construct the reality of that world. (1991: 105-6) [Emphasis mine]

Those who have the power to name often have, by that very act of naming, the power to structure reality, and this power increases dramatically with the degree to which that authority is considered legitimate. Scholars, for example, have such powers, which is the reason why the language of intellectual discourse in any society is particularly important for how the members of that society perceive and structure reality.

As I have already argued, the imposition of a standard variety of speech as the legitimate competence in a society is normally paralleled by the centralization and consolidation of power. Therefore, the competition between varieties or languages in a national polity, or an international context, is really a struggle for symbolic power by different interest groups which could be intranational, or international. In this regard, Bourdieu's summary of the situation which at one time obtained in France is particularly apt:

>...The conflict between the French of the revolutionary intelligentsia and the dialects or *patois* was a struggle for symbolic power in which what was at stake was the *formation* and *reformation* of mental structures. In short, it was not only a question of communicating but of gaining recognition for a new language of authority, with its new political vocabulary, its terms of address and reference, its metaphors, its euphemisms and the representation of the social world which it conveys, and which, because it is linked to the new interest groups, is inexpressible in the local idioms shaped by usages linked to the specific interests of peasant groups. (1991: 47-8)

At various times in the African sociolinguistic context, the lower classes, and occasionally minority groups, are in a position similar to that of the French peasants in the above context. Yet at other times, the entire nations of Africa are in the peasant position in relation to the dominant economies of the West and, as has sometimes been the case, the oil-rich Arab countries of the Middle East. Most of the linguistic debates and international aid in the context of language teaching are all too often strategies in the ongoing historical struggle to institute one's speech as the dominant competence. And since such competence functions as capital it secures for the dominant group tremendous advantages in their interactions in those fields which are considered most crucial for power.

The most important indirect method of continuing the struggle is the power to name, and in consequence, define social reality. As a means of imposing a group's will over others through symbolic violence its effect is dramatic, especially given the fact that unlike most other methods of imposing one's will it is least obvious. Here, the larger struggle is that between the Western world view expressed in the English language and those of indigenous Nigerian cultures. Simply put, the issue is whether the continued use of English is not, in addition to other factors, changing the African social reality that is at the core of the identity of the elite class. In other words, how has the use of language contributed, and is contributing, to the determination of what we have labeled and are describing as African reality? I will advance the argument that, given the differences in the internal dynamics of English and the local Nigerian languages in the way they structure our perception of reality, that is, the reality expressed, and perhaps expressible, in each, our social reality and that of future generations are changing and cannot be called authentically African. To this end, I will compare, briefly, some aspects of the structuring of reality in Yoruba and English, particularly in the areas of cosmology, sex-roles, and kinship.

It is not certain that members of the Westernized elite are themselves conscious soldiers in this struggle, even though the cultural capital they have accumulated in the process of their Westernization positions them exactly where they can derive maximum profit from a resolution of the conflict in favor of English. The conclusion to be drawn here also points in the direction of the ultimate danger in resolving the national language question in favor of any one of the contending forces in Nigeria.

That the Westernized elite which in the Nigerian context most closely approximates the middle class should indeed be at the center of this struggle is not surprising. After all, the middle class has historically constructed its identity via a simultaneous acceptance and rejection of the other. It seeks linguistic assimilation into the higher class and, at the same time, dissimulation, or exclusion, from the lower class. But in the case of Nigeria, the potential dangers in such behavior are grave because, given the inchoate nature of the classes, its influence on the lower classes is indeed great. Consequently, the entire society stand in danger of losing out should the middle class commit significant errors of judgement.

C. Cosmology

Since cosmology underlies all culture it is particularly appropriate for the kind of comparison of cultures which I intended to undertake here. We cannot doubt the fact that a society's pattern of life is an expression of a particular view of man in the context of the universe held by that society. This is significant not only for the organization of secular life, but for religion as well: "The practices of religion are as much the outcome of its [society's] doctrine of God as of its estimate of man. There is a sense in which the doctrine of God can be viewed as an expression of a certain view of man" (Sidhom 1969: 113). Cosmology also represents an area in which there exists the greatest divergence between Africans and the peoples of European descent.

Since central to the question of cosmology is the whole issue of the culturally or religiously determined estimates of man, I will briefly review this issue in Western thought. In this respect, we are confronted with two dominant traditions: the theological and the "scientific". We may identify four major approaches (three of which are clearly theological) to the estimate of man in Western thought:

1. Estimating man on the basis of the Genesis record of man's origin and sin (Cave 1944);
2. The Christ-centered approach (Schleiermacher 1928);
3. The social approach (Niebuhr 1933); and
4. The evolutionary approach (Chardin de 1959).

Regardless of the peculiarities of each of these approaches, the first three at least provide us with an estimate of man rooted in the Judeo-Christian religious beliefs as encapsulated in mainstream Christian theology. According to this theological estimate of man, he is the most important animate creation in this realm, which in fact is the only one besides Heaven and Hell. He is variously described as the child, or servant, of God. The path to harmony is through the acceptance of Jesus Christ, *the Son*--as opposed to *a son*--of God as a personal savior. Man's relationship to other creation is that he is their lord and master.

The other remaining approach to the estimate of man derived from the empirical and rationalist philosophical traditions of Europe and the Darwinian theory of evolution. Since the theory of evolution is so well-known, it does not require further elaboration here. Suffice it to say that, according to that theory, only the fittest survive in the evolutionary process of all species. In a sense, then, the entire world is at war, with only the strong surviving. Even though I have simplified both estimates somewhat, I believe that my representation notes the essential points. The only other point that I wish to make here is that, in reality, the Darwinian estimate has been the basic, guiding cosmological principle of Western civilization, especially as is demonstrated in the ideology of capitalism.

Among the Yoruba we see several myths which represent different traditions concerning explanations of the origin of man (See, for example, Lucas 1948, Parrinder 1953, Bolaji-Idowu 1962, Pay 1976, and Awolalu 1979). Whichever tradition we accept, the major point which comes across is that the Yoruba tradition, like most other African traditions, believe that man was created by God and has his origin in God. However, Africans pragmatically produced no theological systems to frame this belief (Sidhom 1969). This represents my point of departure here, along with the knowledge we gain from the reference to the physical and spiritual entities in Yoruba language. This latter consideration is particularly important given the centrality of language to this inquiry.

In Yoruba cosmology, the entire world is animate. The generic word for all creation is *èdá*. All creations are *omo* (child) to *Olódùmarè* (who has no sexual identity), the Supreme Being and Creator. The lexical category *omo* assumes a sculptural implication: "that which is molded" since the full explication is "*Èdá omo Olódùmarè*"--*Èdá* who is molded by the Creator. Each *omo* has *èmi* (spirit, life) and form.

The sub-sets of *èdá* are *ènìyàn* (humankind), *igi* (trees), *eranko* (animals), *òkè* (hills/mountains), etc. Since each possesses *èmí*, that is, life, the entire world is animate. Furthermore, *èdá* is distinguished on the basis of sex: *ako* (male) and *abo* (female). The fact that we have *ako* and *abo eranko* and *igi*, etc., underscores the animation of the whole of creation.

Humankind's unique position in creation is explained in the meaning of *ènìyàn*:

> *ènìyàn*: *eni-tí-a-yàn* (*eni tí a yàn láti mú rere wá'yé*): the one that is chosen to bring good to the world. (Akiwowo 1986)

After *Olódùmarè* had successfully completed the creation process, *Olódùmarè* chose the human being to lead the entire creation--*èdá*--to this planet. The implication of this is that, on another planet, another creation--for example, the ant--might be the selected leader.

We may now briefly examine the ideological implications of these varying cosmological systems. Yoruba cosmology provides an essentially unified world view. There is unity between all the creations and the Creator, since the former are all *èdá omo Olódùmarè*. Between parent and child, the relationship of love will be expected to hold as well as between the children. There is, therefore, an essential unity of all creation.

Furthermore, all are equal before the Creator. Man's position as *ènìyàn*, the chosen leader, imposes responsibility and accountability on him. He has to treat the entire world, which is animate, with reverence. The mindless and ruthless exploitation not only of *ènìyàn* (fellow human beings), but *eranko, igi*, etc.--that is, the entire environment--which until recently has been largely sanctioned by Western civilization, is not allowed. You take what you *need* and leave the rest. Appiah-Kubi (1981) observes a similar cosmological view among the Akan of Ghana:

> Proper land use is evidence of faithfulness to God and Mother Earth and is reflected in the health of the soil and nature and economic health or prosperity of the society. Unjust land use on the other hand spells social, economic, spiritual disaster, crop failure, and epidemics....Ills are often attributed to the unfaithfulness of the people. The logic here is simply that we cannot expect to do harm and violence to nature and Mother Earth who are the bearers of our life and existence without precipitating crises in our economic, social, spiritual, animal, plant, and human life. (9-10)

English--i.e., Western--cosmology that oscillates between visions of the world as God's creation and as an evolutionary object imposes no comparable responsibility on man. In this cosmology, the unity of all creation is missing. In fact, the lack of animation of most of creation frees man from any strong sense of responsibility and sanctions social and material Darwinism, the ruthless exploitation of man and environment which is the hallmark of capitalism and, to varying degrees, communism. It is no wonder then that all these ideological positions inherent in most African cosmologies were summarily dismissed by Europeans as pagan and primitive beliefs, particularly by the missionaries and their inheritors. Unfortunately, this is still the belief of most people around the world and, tragically, that of many African converts to the religions of Islam, Christianity, and "Science".

The essential point I wish to make here is that, given the other features that characterize the unequal exchange between local and foreign, Western culture, those who grow up using the English language extensively, and often to the exclusion of their mother tongue, are likely to develop an increased tendency to assume the ideological stance of the cosmological underpinning of the English language. I will return to this point after a cursory examination of some other aspects of the categorization of reality in Yoruba and English.

D. Sex-Roles

As I have noted in the discussion of cosmology above, the sexual distinctions of *ako* and *abo* (male and female respectively) runs through the entire spectrum of *eda* (creation). I am, however, focusing my comparison of Yoruba and English on the specification of sex-roles in the two.

In Yoruba, the generic word for human beings is *èniyàn*. *Èniyàn*, in terms of sex, could be *ako* (*okùnrin*--male) or *abo* (*obìnrin*--female). This is in contrast to English which has the generic term, man, which could be either male (man) or female (woman). The schema is given below:

	Yoruba		**English**	
	èniyàn		man	
ako		*abo*	male	female
okùnrin		*obìnrin*	man	woman
(òdómokùnrin)		*(òdómobìnrin)*	(boy)	(girl)

The schema above represents how Yoruba and English subcategorize the phenomenon of sex in both languages. The use of the label for one of the sexes-- *man*--as a generic term in English, it has been argued, implies, or reinforces a male-sexist ideological position in English which is not reflected in Yoruba. This sexist position runs through the entire lexicon of English and has attracted the attention of several scholars (See, for example, Nilsen 1973, Blakar 1979, Penelope 1991). For example, Nilsen has observed that many words once associated with women automatically become pejorative:

call girl (= prostitute)	vs. *call* boy
madam (brothel manager)	vs. Sir
mistress (concubine)	vs. master
spinster (= old maid)	vs. bachelor
witch	vs. wizard (+ wisdom)

Of course, the language is also replete with words that indicate it is a man's world: *masterplan*, and not **mistressplan*, *kingdom* and not **queendom*, etc. Certainly, there are problems with using language structure and lexical categories exclusively as clues to the sexist or non-sexist nature of the cultures behind languages. For example, while the Turkish language will be considered "non-sexist," certainly noone will deny that Turkish society is decidedly patriarchal and sexist.

The area of grammatical categories sheds further light on this sexist ideological characteristic of English grammar. We may note in this respect the grammatical category of gender. Yoruba lacks this category, while English has three genders--generally now natural and retained in the pronominal system. Although there are still some relics of the old, elaborate gender system of English in the pronouns used for some nouns (e.g., the use of "it" for a child, "she" for a ship, etc.), it is the gender specifically indicated in the third personal, singular pronouns in English that have been the subject of criticism for their alleged sexism:

Singular

Masculine: he }

Feminine: she} + their case and number
derivatives.

Neuter: it }

Yoruba employs only the gender-neutral pronoun "ó" for all three, in addition to having case and number derivatives. Of course, since the generic term in English is masculine the generic pronoun is also *he*. In Yoruba with a sexually unmarked generic term, *ènìyàn*, the pronoun is "ó" which is equally unmarked for sex. It is perhaps interesting to note that even the *òrìsà* (deity/gods and goddesses) in Yoruba cosmology share in this gender-blending. In terms of those properties which in another culture might tend to be associated with different sexes, we observe an interesting phenomenon. One of the properties used to classify the orisa is temperament. Accordingly, we have *òrìsà gbìgbóná* ("hot" *òrìsà*, i.e. temperamental gods/goddesses) and *òrìsà funfun* ("cool, temperate, symbolically white" *òrìsà*). Counted in the ranks of the *òrìsà gbìgbóná* are *Oya* (*Sàngó's* wife and queen of the whirlwind), *Obalúayé* ("lord of pestilence") *Ògún*, and *Sàngó*. These are harsh, demanding, aggressive, and quick-tempered gods and goddesses. *Òrìsà oko, Obàtálá,* and *Òsanyìn* ("lord of leaves and medicine")--all male, and *Olókun* (goddess of the sea), *Yemoja*, and *Òsun*--all female, are examples of *òrìsà funfun* (Drewal, Pemberton, and Abiodun 1989).

The social power which language exerts in this area of power constellation is quite significant. As Blakar (1971, 1973) has demonstrated for Norwegian--and this holds for English as well--language structuring here reflects and conserves the existing sex-role pattern, even to the extent of counteracting change. In fact, as children grow up they do both directly and indirectly learn their traditional sex-roles as they acquire their mother tongue. I am aware of the fact that my suggestions about the degrees of sexism present in English (and Western culture) and Yoruba (and Yoruba culture) runs counter to the grain of popular and supposed social "scientific" knowledge. But the fact is that, while the Yoruba like several other groups might be guilty of some sexism, the picture normally presented in Western media and often reinforced by Western scholars (e.g., Stageman 1974, and Frank 1984) is severely flawed. One example often cited in support of the thesis of African male sexism is the existence of polygyny. But the conclusions often reflect a characteristic Western attitude of glossing over the variations in African cultures, as well as a fundamental failure to really understand how several African societies defined social roles. In most African structuring of social roles, kinship is central. And in several African societies--for example, among the Yoruba--of the two ways in which women relate to men--that is, as sister and as wives--the more important is the first (as sisters). The role of a wife is not only considered inferior and with less power, but it is also not considered to be necessarily permanent (that is, not "until Death do us part"). It is not unusual for women to return to their family home when they are past child-bearing, and they are also often buried there. In addition, women traditionally inherit, not from their husbands, but from their own siblings. What is important then is that society establishes clear responsibilities for both the male and the female in their roles as husbands and wives--something which traditional African societies did very clearly, and not necessarily to the total disadvantage of women.

Unfortunately, all too often we find African scholars who should know better echoing Western views, as the following statement illustrates:

The advent of colonialism and the attendant spread of Western culture with its acceptance of women's basic equality with men changed ...[the second class status of women]...Today, while there are still pockets of hard-core male chauvinism women compete more favorably with men and are being slowly accepted as men's equals... (Oladeji 1987: 112)

Nothing could be further from the truth. As several historians have noted, while the colonial experience in Africa might be considered a mixed blessing in some respects, the fate of women in society certainly wasn't one of those supposed blessings. For the African woman, it was a clear disaster. Walter Rodney in his seminal work on colonialism in Africa explains its effect on them thus:

> What happened to African women under colonialism is that the social, religious, constitutional, and political privileges and rights disappeared... When [the men] were required to leave their farms to seek employment, women remained behind burdened with every task necessary for the survival of themselves, the children, and even the men as far as foodstuffs were concerned. Moreover, since men entered the money sector more easily and in greater numbers than women, women's work became greatly inferior to that of men within the new value system of colonialism: men's work was "modern" and women's was "traditional" and "backward". (1974: 227)

Even societies such as the Akan and Dahomey in West Africa that were matriarchal were virtually turned around as a Europe that was at the high point of Victorian sexism ravaged and pillaged the African continent. (See ,also, Bay 1991 and Goke-Pariola 1991).

In the Nigerian situation, given the increasing primacy of English over the indigenous languages, the acquisition and use of English cannot but encourage and accelerate the socialization of children into what--contrary to popular Western belief--is a more sharply defined male dominance configuration pattern as reflected in English. In other words, they grow up accepting and preserving the sexism of a Western social reality.

E. Kinship Terminology

One more area of human experience which reflects the powerful relationship between language and ideology, or the structuring of reality, is kinship. This is particularly important because the classification is one of a basic part of human experience--man's relationship with others in his immediate social environment. I have tried below to present a brief outline of Yoruba and English kinship terms.

In all probability, the first list below, that is, the one for Yoruba, cannot be considered exhaustive; nevertheless, it suffices for the purposes of illustration here. It gives the Yoruba kinship terms in addition to some of the kin-types to which each refers. These kin-types indicate kinsmen who fill genealogical positions in the set of all kinsmen reckoned from some particular individual as a point of reference. The key to the abbreviations used is as follows: **Mo**, mother (or mother's); **Fa**, father; **Br**, brother; **Si**, sister; **Hu**, husband; **Wi**, wife; **So**, son; **Da**, daughter; **E**, elder; **Y**, younger; ♂, male speaker; ♀, female speaker (the absence of ♂ or ♀ indicates equal use of the term by both sexes).

Bàbá:	Fa; FaFa; FaFaFa; FaBr; MoFa;
	MoFaFa; MoBr; EBr; ♀HuFa;
	♂WiFa; ♀HuFaBr.
Ìyá:	Mo; MoMo; MoMoMo; FaMo; FaMoMo; FaSi;
	MoSi; ESi; ♀HuWWi; ♂WiMo; ♂WiMoSi.
Ọmọ:	OSo;ODa; YFaSo; YFaDa; SoSo; SoDa; DaSo;
	DaDa; YBrSo; YBrDa; YSiSo; YSiDa
Ẹ̀gbọ́n:	EFaSo; EFaDa; EFaWiSo; EFaWiDa; EFaBrSo;
	EFaBrDa; EFaSiSo; EFaSiDa; EMoSiSo;
	EMoSiDa;
	EBrSo; EBrDa; ESiSo; ESiDa.
Àbúrò:	YFaSo; YFaDa; YFaWiSo; YFaWiDa; YFaBrSo;
	YFaBrDa;YFaSiSo; YFaSiDa;YMoSiSo; YMoSiDa;
	YSiSo; YSiDa.
Ìyàwó:	♂Wi; FaWi; FaBrWi; BrWi; ♀HuWi...
Ọkọ:	♀Hu; ♀HuBr...
Àna:	♂WiFa; ♂WiMo...; BrWiFa; BrWiMo...; SiHu...;
	SiHuBr...; ♀HuFa; ♀HuMo...; BrHuFa; BrHuMo;
	SiWi....;

It is to be noted that the first five terms--*Bàbá, Ìyá, Ọmọ, Ẹ̀gbọ́n*, and *Àbúrò*--refer to basically consanguineal kinsfolk, while the last three--*Ìyàwó, Ọkọ*, and *Àna*--are basically affinal. Sometimes, the adjective *kékeré* (small or younger) and *àgbà* (old or elder) are added to the consanguineal terms to signify the age/generation distance from the ego. These consanguineal terms also cover up to the third generation from ego. It would appear that age is basically the most important parameter for defining kinship, with the addition of the basic sex categorization.

The basic schema for English consanguineal relationships that is outlined below has been extrapolated from Burling's (1970) presentation of the American kinship system. In a table that illustrates the schema presented below (Burling 1970), the generations are distributed along the vertical axis and collateral distance along the horizontal axis, with the various categories of terms forming concentric sets around the ego. This, then, presents us with a concept of genealogical distance that combines both generational and collateral distance, with ego himself at zero degree of genealogical distance.

Burling lists the kinship terms for consanguineal relatives up to three generations removed from the ego. At the farthest distance on the plus (that is, older) side are a person's great grandparents. These are three generations removed from ego, from whom they are at a zero degree of collateral distance.

Next are first cousins twice-removed, great uncles and aunts, as well as grandparents. While relatives in this group are two generations removed from ego, in terms of degree of genealogical distance they, along with the grandparents, would be considered second generation family members. One generation removed from ego are first and second cousins once-removed, uncles and aunts, and ego's parents. At a zero degree of genealogical distance from ego are first-, second- and third cousins, brothers, and sisters, who are also in the same generation.

Among the younger relatives who are closest to a person are first and second cousins once-removed, nephews and nieces. Also in this category we find ego's sons and daughters. All these relatives are one generation removed from ego. Next are first cousins twice-removed, grand nephews, and grandchildren. Finally, at three generations away from ego we find great grandchildren.

With regard to affinal relationships, the English (American) terms for the closest are *husband* and *wife*. Like ego himself, the people to whom these two terms refer are at a zero degree of genealogical distance. English indicates other affinal relationships by combining any of the terms for consanguineal kinsmen. Thus, we have terms such as *brother-in-law*; *sister-in-law*; *father-in-law*, etc.

As anyone even minimally familiar with contemporary American culture and society today would note, this picture is certainly far from complete. American society, like most other Western societies, has undergone tremendous cultural changes in the last two decades. Not least among these are the changing structures of the family, principally as a consequence of higher divorce rates and remarriage, as well as differing sexual orientations. Yet, one can claim that, overall, the semantic distinctions made among kinsmen are those of consanguinity, generational location of marriage bond, genealogical distance, sex, and affinal relationship.

From the specification of kinship terminology above, the differences between Yoruba and English in the structuring of family relationships are obvious. Yoruba's use of fewer terms to cover such wide areas and types of relationship demonstrates what constitutes, essentially, a unified frame of relationship--what has been described as the "extended family". In this respect, the Yoruba are again fairly typical of Africans in general. If we were to sum up the cosmological ideology of Africans, we would have to describe it as "existence-in-relation" (Sidhom 1969). It encompasses within its boundaries virtually the entire universe. English, on the other hand, makes finer distinctions and thus fragmentizes this part of reality.

The implications of this observation for ideology are enormous. Even the employment of the term "extended family" by Nigerians when they wish to refer to family members beyond the Western nuclear family is dangerous; it presumes that the Western model is the norm, and the traditional African system the deviation. But what other outcome can we expect given the years of formal schooling in English and the pervasive indoctrination into a Western world view through religion, the mass media, and popular culture via the medium of English? Had Africans retained their languages, they would perhaps have had little cause to refer to their families as "extended".

The use of a particular kinship term implies a subscription to a particular cultural ideology. It imposes certain obligations on the addressor and addressee, or frees them from others. That is to say, the semantic load which kinship terms carry are significant for behavior and social interaction. To be called *bàbá* as opposed to *uncle* imposes a higher sense of responsibility on both interlocutors. Similarly, to be called an *àna* is not semantically and culturally equivalent to being called an *in-law*. Similarly, when a woman calls her *brother-in-law* "*oko mi*" (my husband), it imposes virtually all the responsibilities of the husband on the addressee and that of the wife on the addressor. Only sex is primarily excluded.

The Yoruba like most other Africans tend to view life as a structure of roles and functions. For example, the term "father" (*bàbá*) as used in Africa applies, generally,

...not only to the immediate father, the procreator, but also to
paternal uncles and all the men of the clan of the father's age-group.
Being a father, or an uncle, each by itself, is a distinct role, to fulfill
a certain distinct function in society, and carries with it certain
obligations and rights. (Sidhom 1969: 108)

This also applies to political titles: the king, the chief, and the elder, for example,
have the function of preserving the integrity of the community and guarding its
peace and security.

The sense of communalism implied in these kinship terms is critical to
African social organization. The English language takes the ideological position of
fragmentation of reality and distancing of relationships. This is the whole point
about language and ideology: that each language presupposes a particular
ideology--as opposed to physical reality--which is reflected both in its lexical and
grammatical categories; therefore, to acquire a language and to use it extensively
in daily life, including very intimate aspects of individual and community life, is to
subscribe to that particular ideology. The ultimate culmination is the development
of individualism without social responsibility. On the other hand, the ideology of
Yoruba kinship terminology is one of social responsibility. The individual defines
himself in relation to the others in his immediate social world to whom he owes an
obligation and who, in turn, are obliged to reciprocate. Given the effects of
Western contact, no longer will individuals define themselves in relation to others
in their social environment in terms of reciprocal obligations.

From the admittedly inexhaustive discussion of the different ways in which
Yoruba and English categorize experience--both lexically and grammatically--it is
obvious that the use of the two languages ultimately imposes on the users a
different structuring of reality. Children who grow up using the English language
are, therefore, further socialized into assuming the ideological position of the
English language in respect of how the world is to be experienced and related to.
The use of English in a sense implies a change in the social conventions which
underline our use of speech and, consequently, a change in our apprehension of
reality.

Of course, it is not just the interest of Western societies which are
advanced by this symbolic conflict. A sizable percentage of the Westernized elite
which seeks to free itself from the obligations of traditional life has a vested

interest in promoting English and the ideology it symbolically represents. There are many who seek the goals of individuality without social responsibility and therefore want to be *uncles* rather than *fathers*, or *nephews* rather than *sons*, and *brothers-in-law* rather than *husbands*. And they find powerful allies in the new institutions such as the Christian church which preaches abandonment of the old ways in favor of the new. It should be noted that it also further distances them from the lower class, which is closest to tradition, an "elite closure" which helps maintain for them and their offspring their hold on power. Similarly, those nationalities that are busy promoting their languages as the future "official" or "national" language of the nation also have their eyes on the ultimate prize: the ability to impose their vision of social reality on others.

F. Conclusion

Both the colonial and post colonial linguistic situation in Nigeria, and indeed the vast majority of African countries, thus confirm the thesis that symbolic violence is a potent weapon with which to impose one's will and maintain the legitimacy of that power. Pierre Bourdieu has correctly defined symbolic power as:

... a power of constituting the given through utterances, of making people see and believe, of conforming or transforming the vision of the world, and thereby, action on the world and thus the world itself, an almost magical power which enables one to obtain the equivalent of what is obtained through force (whether physical or economic)... (1991: 170)

This power is most effective because both those who benefit from its exercise as well as those who are dominated by it are largely unaware of what the real issues are. Africans thus engage themselves arguing about "national" and "official" languages, when the real issue has, more often than not, been *Who will accumulate and maintain the most power in society?*

As the discussion of language and ideology above would suggest, the implications of the symbolic struggle in African societies and elsewhere go far beyond national boundaries. In explaining his structural sociology of language whose object is "the relationship between the structured systems of social differences," Bourdieu makes the claim that "the process of unification of both the production and circulation of economic and cultural goods entails the progressive obsolescence of the earlier mode of production of the habitus and its products" (1991: 50). Although he made the statement within the context of a nation, it is equally applicable to the current international economic context of the centralization of power (a.k.a. "globalized economy"). In this context, then, African languages and the indigenous constructions of social reality as they are reflected in, for example, kinship terminology, cosmology, and sex-roles, are the obsolete means. Thus we see a dramatic example of the continuation of the struggles in the political economy by symbolic means, a means whose gains are dramatically significant given the absence of physical violence.

The observations I have made so far fall into two categories. The first concerns the power differential between English, on the one hand, and the indigenous languages on the other in national life and its implications for the African reality Africans seek to describe and live, as well as that of the parameters which are used for its interpretation. The second is in respect of the ideological implications of the internal dynamics of English as opposed to that of local languages as systems of structuring reality, and the implications of the differences for the contemporary and future African social reality. In respect of power, in most domains of Nigerian national life such as education, religion, popular culture and the political economy, English exhibits a distinctive dominance configuration pattern while the indigenous languages operate from a position of marked weakness. In fact, the direction of the future is clear: More and more, parents are specifying English as the language they would want their children to know best.

In a world whose many domains are increasingly governed by English, a Western, non-native language, besides the socio-economic and political problems that arise, can the social reality continue to evolve as African? Indigenous languages are daily losing more and more power to English. Rodney has underscored the importance of the equation of power in relationships between societies and cultures:

> Power is the ultimate determinant in human society, being basic to the relations within any group and between groups. It implies the ability to defend one's interests and if necessary to impose one's will by any means available. In relations between peoples, the question of power determines maneuverability in bargaining, the extent to which one people respect the interests of another, and eventually

the extent to which a people survive as a physical and cultural entity. (1973: 24)

Since language is a means, or vehicle, of power, the loss of language itself is, to a significant extent, the loss of power and the loss of cultural originality and initiative. It is obvious that a people whose world is increasingly governed by an alien language, especially one that they have lacked the will to completely indigenize both formally and ideologically, cannot continue the process of cultural evolution along their own lines. Therefore, like other factors in cultural invasion language us distorts social reality. Furthermore, with a consciousness developed in English as a medium of intellectual discourse, the parameters used in the interpretation of African reality cannot be reliable. The sum total of both trends is a theorizing using data that is inauthentic and is arrived at on the basis of false premises.

In respect of ideology we confront a more serious problem. Given the fact that no language is ideologically neutral in terms of the way it structures reality, the continued extensive use of English will ultimately lead to a negative change in how Africans perceive their social reality. Africans will eventually assume a Western sociopolitical structure and adopt the position of a particular segment of Western, or in reaction--as some virtually did--an equally alien Eastern, ideology. Fanon (1963) also makes a similar point. He argues that "Third World" countries should reject the notion that they must define themselves principally on the basis of those (Western) nations that have preceded them. "Third World" countries need not assume that the choice which confronts them is a life and death one between capitalism on the one hand, and socialism on the other, no matter how these ideologies have been defined. Rather, they ought to reach within their own souls, their past as peoples, for the values that would determine how they progress in their own evolution.

Lacking such a radical and truly independent understanding of the imperative before them, and having lost their language and their voice, many African intellectuals perceive their tasks to be ultimately no more than the replication of the patterns that have been identified in other worlds. They end up eventually with false theories about a fake entity which they call African. The working of this aspect is indeed more subtle than the first, and its effects are less readily discerned. But they are present and very potent.

We do in fact see this problem if we consider aspects of African social reality other than those we have examined here. They are also thrown into bold relief when we consider the fact that English is not only a language of day-to-day reference and social interaction within and outside the family, but is also the primary, if not exclusive, medium of intellectual discourse. This carries the further implication that most scholars will automatically lapse into their discourse and analyses using non-indigenous categories. These intellectual categories cover all areas of academic discourse, ranging from linguistics, economics, political science, public administration, medicine, the law and religion, to social anthropology. They affect not only the kinds of kinship terminology that I have discussed above but even the basic consanguineal institution of marriage.

It might seem obvious to us that we understand what a marriage is, for example. But that is really only if we start from the same understanding of this social anthropological conceptual category. However, as Isichei (1987) clearly demonstrates, if we take the Western definition of the category "marriage" as our starting point, we would definitely have to exclude several types of co-habitational and other arrangements which the Anaguta of Nigeria, for example, consider to be normal parts of the socially sanctioned procreation process in their society.

Isichei documents "five institutions through which paired heterosexuals may indulge in procreative sex": "*ndumaina*,"--"a legal friend"; "*bukhelelei*"--"the capture or enticement by a youth of a maid"; "*rigissau*"--"a rite through which a pair of heterosexuals are publicly authorized to live together after obtaining adult status"; "*anya-amashira*"--"the sexual exchange of sisters for the purpose of living together by adults who have successfully gone through <u>Ndumaina</u>, <u>Bukhelelei</u> and <u>Rigissau</u>"; and "rendele"--"the capture or seduction of a woman who is another's <u>anya-amashira</u>" (1987: 2).

Our error in this regard would of course have important legal as well as social consequences on the multi-ethnic and multicultural society that Nigeria is today, not to mention the international context. The variety in the range of categories that the Yoruba and other Africans classify as part of the institution of marriage is similarly instructive. As Isichei himself admits, as a Western-trained social anthropologist and outsider to the Anaguta culture, he was confused by "the fact that [his] informants used the term marriage to apply to each of their five institutions: <u>ndumaina</u>, <u>bukhelelei</u>, <u>rigissau</u>, <u>anya-amashira</u> and <u>rendele</u>" (1987: 10).

Isichei sums up the problems caused by the medium or mode of intellectual discourse thus: "We cannot be politically independent without intellectual independence" (1987: 18).

One cannot overstate this last point which, as already discussed in Chapter Two, is rooted in the colonial experience, and which remains central to the national crises in several previously colonized African countries. According to Chinweizu (1988),

> ...the central aspect of the colonial mentality consists in its keeping us beholden to the authority of alien traditions, alien definitions and alien outlooks. When people are afflicted with such mental servitude, it is difficult for them to look at their reality with clear eyes or to focus their attention on their vital interests. (7)

The institution and perpetuation of English as the preeminent medium of education, social interaction, and intellectual discourse is key to this problem. This point is also succinctly made by Akiwowo (1988):

> Social reality is one, but consciousness of it is many. Our languages, whichever they may be, play determining roles in our consciousness and in the determination of our social reality....it is the development and internalisation of Western European languages which had enabled them to transmit their oral traditions to all mankind. This transmission had resulted in historic adjustments in mental outlooks among Africans, Asians, Mayans, and Slavs, to mention a few among the world's language groups and races who had received the influence of the English language. (46-7)

Already, many scholars take the position that English is no longer the language of the English (e.g. Kachru 1976, 1982, Mazrui 1974, Achebe 1966). Such scholars talk about the "nativization" of English in non-English countries. While you can modify the English language in everyday use to some extent--as some like Chinua Achebe have done in creative writing--the problems raised in the areas of cosmology and kinship, for example, will remain, as will the fundamental problem inherent in its use as the medium of intellectual discourse. As for those of us in Africa, we need to realign power in favor of indigenous languages and cultures in order to ensure the recognition of African thoughts, concepts and ideas which are congruent with our empirical world--*igbésí ayé wa* (Akiwowo 1988), in preference to those which are alien, no matter what local flavor we may have added to them.

BIBLIOGRAPHY

Abdulaziz, M. H. 1971. Tanzania's National Language Policy and the Rise of Swahili Political Culture. In W. H. Whiteley (ed.), *Language Use and Social Change*, London: Oxford University Press for the International African Institute, 160-178.

_____1980. The Ecology of Tanzanian National Language Policy. In E. C. Polomé and C. P. Hill (eds.), *Language in Tanzania*, London: Oxford University Press for the International African Institute, 139-175.

Abernethy, D. B. 1969. *The Political Dilemma of Popular Education: An African Case*. Stanford: Stanford University Press.

Abubakar, S. 1980. The Northern Provinces Under Colonial Rule. In O. Ikime (ed.), *Groundwork of Nigerian History*, Ibadan: Heinemann Educational Books & Historical Society of Nigeria, 447-481.

Achebe, C. 1966. The English Language and the African Writer. *Insight* October/December.

Afigbo, A. E. 1980. The Eastern Provinces under Colonial Rule. In Ikime (ed.), *Groundwork of Nigerian History*, 410-428.

Afolayan, A. A. 1979. The English Language and Political and Educational Ideologies for Nigeria. Paper presented at the Meeting of the Ifeversity English Students Society, University of Ife, Ile-Ife.

African National Congress (ANC). 1991. *Discussion Document: Constitutional Principles for a Democratic South Africa*. Johannesburg: ANC Constitutional Committee

_____1992. *African National Congress Language Policy Considerations*. Johannesburg: ANC Department of Arts and Culture.

Akinnaso, F. N. 1987. Language Planning and Political Development in Nigeria. Paper presented at the University Roundtable, University of Wisconsin-Parkside, 5 October, 1987.

_____1989. One nation, Four Hundred Languages: Unity and Diversity in Nigeria's Language Policy. *Language Problems and Language Planning* 13(2): 133-146.

Akiwowo, A. A. 1986. Committing the Contributions of an African Oral Tradition to the Peace Process. Paper presented at the Seminar on "World

Peace--Contributions, Commitment and Attitude," organized by the Bahai Group, University of Ife, Ile-Ife, June 11, 1986.

_____1988. Indigenizing the Social Sciences and Emancipation of Thought: A Valedictory Lecture delivered at Obafemi Awolowo University, Ile-Ife, Nigeria, August 18, 1988.

Alatas, S. H. 1977. *The Myth of the Lazy Native*. London: Frank Cass and Company.

Allan, K. 1978. Nation, Tribalism and National Language: Nigeria's Case. *Cahiers d'Etudes Africaines* 18: 397-415.

Ambrose, S. 1982. Archaeology and Linguistic Reconstruction in East Africa. In C. Ehret & M. Ponansky (eds.) *The Archaeological and Linguistic Reconstruction of African History*, Berkeley and Los Angeles: University of California Press, 104-57.

Appiah-Kubi, K. 1981. *Man Cures, God Heals*. New York: Friendship Press.

Asiwaju, A. I. 1980. The Western Provinces under Colonial Rule. In Ikime (ed.), *Groundwork of Nigerian History*, 429-446.

Atkinson, R. 1985. 'State' Formation and Language Change in Westernmost Acholi in the Eighteenth Century. In A. I. Salim (ed.), *State Formation in Eastern Africa*, New York: St. Martin's Press, 91-125.

Awolalu, J. O. 1979. *Yoruba Beliefs and Sacrificial Rites*. London: Longman.

Awoniyi, T. A. 1975. The Yoruba Language and the Formal School System: A Study of the Colonial Language Policy in Nigeria. *Journal of Educational Administration and History* VII (2): 9-19.

Ayandele, E. A. 1974. *The Educated Elite in Nigerian Society*. Ibadan: Ibadan University Press.

_____1980. External Relations with Europeans in the Nineteenth Century: Explorers, Missionaries and Traders. In Ikime (ed.), *Groundwork of Nigerian History*, 367-389.

Barnard, F. M. (ed.). 1969. *Herder on Social and Political Thought*. Cambridge: Cambridge University Press.

Barton, H. D. 1980. Language Use Among Ilala Residents. In Polome and Hill (eds.), *Language in Tanzania*, 176-205.

Bay, E. 1991. African Women and Contact with the West: The Case of Dahomey. Lecture delivered at Georgia Southern University, Statesboro, Georgia,

October 16, 1991.

Bee, H. et al. 1969. Social Class Differences in Maternal Teaching Strategies and Speech Patterns. *Developmental Psychology* I(6): 726-734.

Bernstein, B. 1961. Social Class and Linguistic Development: A Theory of Social Learning. In A. H. Halsey et al (eds.), *Education, Economy, and Society.* New York: Free Press.

Bird, C. 1970. The Development of Mandekan (Manding): A Study of the Role of Extra-Linguistic Factors in Linguistic Change. In D. Dalby (ed.), *Language and History in Africa*, London: Cass, 146-159.

Blakar, R. M. 1973b. Context-effects and Coding Stations in Sentence Processing. *Scandinavian Journal of Psychology* 14: 103-105.

_____1979. Language as a Means of Social Power. In J. L. Mey (ed.), *Pragmalinguistics*, The Hague: Mouton.

Blakar, R. M. & R. Rommetveit. 1971. Processing of Utterances in Contexts versus Learning of Sentences: Some Pilot Studies and a Design for an Experiment. In E. A. Carswell & R. Rommetveit (eds.), *Social Contexts of Messages*, London: Academic Press.

Bokamba, E. G. 1976. Authenticity and the Choice of a National Language: The Case of Zaire. *Studies in the Linguistic Sciences* 6: 23-64.

_____1984. French Colonial Language Policy in Africa and Its Legacies. *Studies in the Linguistic Sciences* 14: 1-35.

Bolaji-Idowu, E. 1962. *Olodumare: God in Yoruba Belief.* London: Longman.

_____1975. *African Traditional Religion.* New York: Orbis Books.

Bourdieu, P. 1991. *Language and Symbolic Power.* Cambridge, Mass.: Harvard University Press.

Bowcock, D. 1985. Educational Language Planning in the Gambia. Ph.D. Dissertation, University of Wisconsin. University Microfilms: MBP8516756.

Brann, C. M. B. 1977. The Role of Language in Nigeria's Educational Policy. *The Nigerian Language Teacher* I(2): 32-38.

Bretton, H. L. 1976. Political Science, Language, and Politics. In W. M. O'Barr and J. F. O'Barr (eds.), *Language and Language*, The Hague: Mouton, 431-48.

Bridgland, F. 1991. More than a language learning experience... *The Star*, October

21, 1991: 9.

Brosnahan, J. F. 1965. Some Historical Cases of Language Imposition. In J. Spencer (ed.), *Language in Africa*, Cambridge: Cambridge University Press.

Burling, R. 1970. *Man's Many Voices*. New York: Holt, Rinehart and Winston Inc.

Buxton, C. 1848. *Memoirs of Sir Thomas Fowell Buxton*. London: John Murray.

Cameron, D. 1990. Demythologizing Sociolinguistics: Why Language Does not Reflect Society. In J. E. Joseph and T. J. Taylor (eds.), *Ideologies of Language*. London & New York: Routledge, 79-93.

Cameron, J. and W. A. Dodd. 1970. *Society, School and Progress in Tanzania*, Oxford: Pergamon Press/Oxford University Press.

Cave, S. 1944. *The Christian Estimate of Man*. London: Duckworth.

Champion, J. 1969. Native Languages Suggested for African Education. *Le Monde*, Paris, December 3, 1969: 9, 11.

Chardin de, P. T. 1959. *The Phenomenon of Man*. London: Collins.

Chinweizu. 1975. *The West and the Rest of Us*. New York: Vintage Books.

_____1988. Why Decolonize the African Mind? "The Chinweizu Observatory", *Sunday Vanguard* (Lagos), May 1, 1988: 7.

Chinweizu, C. Madubuike, and O. Jemie. 1980. *Toward the Decolonization of African Literature, Vol. 1*. Enugu: Fourth Dimension Publishers.

Chomsky, N. 1965. *Aspects of the Theory of Syntax*. Cambridge, Mass.: MIT Press.

Coleman, J. S. (ed.). 1965. *Education and Political Development*. Princeton: Princeton University Press.

D'Encause, H. C. 1978. *L'Empire éclat*. Flammarion, Paris: Livre de Poche, 5433.

Dakin, J., B. Tiffen, and A. G. Widdowson. 1968. *Language in Education*. London: Oxford University Press.

Devitt, M., and K. Sterelny. 1987. *Language and Reality: An Introduction to the Philosophy of Language*. Cambridge, Mass.: MIT Press.

Drewal, J. D., J. Pemberton, and R. Abiodun. 1989. *YORUBA: Nine Centuries of African Art and Thought*. New York: The Center for African Art & Henry N. Abrams, Inc.

Dubow, F. 1976. Language, Law, and Change: Problems in the Development of a

National Legal System in Tanzania. In O'Barr and O'Barr (eds.), *Language and Politics*, 85-99.

Eggert, J. 1970. *Missionsschule und sozialer Wandel in Ostafrika.* Bertelsmann Universitätsverlag.

Fafunwa, B. A. 1974. *History of Education in Nigeria.* London: George Allen and Unwin Ltd.

Fanon, F. 1963. *The Wretched of the Earth.* New York: Grove Press.

———1967. *Black Skin White Mask.* New York: Grove Press.

Feagans, L., and D. C. Farran (eds.). 1982. *The Language of Children Reared in Poverty.* New York: Academic Press.

Ferguson, C. A. 1959. Diglossia. *Word* 15: 325-340.

Fishman, J. 1968a. Nationality-nationalism and Nation-nationism. In J. Fishman, C. Ferguson, and J. Das Gupta (eds.), *Language Problems of Developing Nations.* New York: John Wiley and Sons, 39-52.

———1968b. Sociolinguistics and the Language Problems of Developing Countries. In Fishman, Ferguson, and Das Gupta (eds.), *Language Problems of Developing Nations*, 3-16.

———1986. Bilingualism and Separatism. *Annals of the American Academy of Political and Social Science* 487 (Sept. 1986): 169-180.

Frank, K. Feminist Criticism and the African Novel. In E. D. Jones and E. Palmer (eds.), *African Literature Today* 14, London and New York: Heinemann/Africana, 34-48.

Freire, P. 1980. *Education for Critical Consciousness.* New York: The Continuum Publishing Corporation.

Gani-Ikilama, T. O. 1990. Use of Nigerian Pidgin in Education: Why Not? In E. N. Emenanjo (ed.), *Multilingualism, Minority Languages and Language Policy in Nigeria*, Agbor: Central Books.

Goke-Pariola, A. 1984. The Sociocultural Dimensions of English Language Pedagogy in Nigeria. *Lagos Review of English Studies* (LARES) VI/VII: 97-111.

———1985. The Political Content of Language Education in Nigeria. *ODU: A Journal of West African Studies* 27: 54-65.

———1987. Toward a Description of the Sociolinguistic Bases of Language Choice in Nigerian Urban Centres. *Ife Studies in English Language*

I(1&2): 87-98.

_____1991. 'The Novelist as Teacher': Myth and the Redefinition of Womanhood in Chinua Achebe's Novels. Paper presented at the 15th Annual Meeting of the Philological Association of the Carolinas, University of North Carolina, Charlotte, February 28-March 2, 1991.

Goody, J. 1986. *The Logic of Writing and the Organization of Society.* Cambridge: Cambridge University Press.

Gorman, T. P. 1970. Language Policy in Kenya. Paper presented to the Language Association of Eastern Africa, Conference on Language for Development, Nairobi.

Halliday M. A. K. 1978. *Language as Social Semiotic: The Social Interpretation of Language and Meaning.* London: Edward Arnold.

Hansford, K., J. Bendor-Samuel, and J. Stanford. 1976. *The Index of Nigerian Languages.* (Studies in Nigerian Languages). Zaria: Ahmadu Bello University Press.

Hawkes, T. 1977. *Structuralism and Semiotics.* London: Methuen.

Henderson, L. 1979. *Angola: Five Centuries of Conflict.* Ithaca, NY.: Cornell University Press.

Herder, J. G. 1772. Essay on the Origin of Language. In Barnard (ed.), *Herder on Social and Political Culture.*

Hess, R., and V. Shipmann. 1965. Early Experience and Socialization of Cognitive Modes in Children. *Child Development* 36: 869-886.

Hilliard, F. H. 1957. *A Short History of Education in British West Africa.* London: Thomas Nelson & Sons Ltd.

Hisket, M. 1975. *History of Hausa Islamic Verse.* London: University of London Press.

Hymes, D. 1977. *Foundations in Linguistics: An Ethnographic Approach.* London: Tavistock.

Isichei, P. A. C. 1987. Procreation in Anaguta and Anthropological Categories: The Problem. Paper presented at the Ife Social Sciences Forum in Honour of Professor Akinsola Akiwowo at the University of Ife, Ile-Ife, February 24, 1987.

Jinadu, L. A. 1976. Language and Politics: On the Cultural Basis of Colonialism. *Cahier d'etude africaines* XVI(3-4).

Joseph, J. E., and T. J. Taylor (eds.). 1990. *Ideologies of Language.*

Jumbam, K. 1980. *The White Man of God.* London: Heinemann Educational Books.

Kachru, B. B. (ed.). 1982. *The Other Tongue: English Across Cultures.* Urbana, IL: University of Illinois Press.

Kaniki, M. H. Y. 1974. TANU - The Party of Independence and National Consolidation. In G. Ruhumbika (ed.), *Towards Ujamaa.* Nairobi: East African Literature Bureau.

Kleiven, J. 1973. Verbal Communication and Intensity of Delivery. *Scandinavian Journal of Psychology* 14:111-113.

Kozelka, P. 1984. The Development of National Languages: A Case Study of Language Planning in Togo. Ph.D. dissertation, Stanford University. University Microfilms: MBP84-20572.

Lafall, J. 1966. *Pathological and Normal Language.* New York: Russell Sage.

Laitin, D. D. 1992. *Language Repertoires and State Construction in Africa.* Cambridge: Cambridge University Press.

Lasswell, H. 1958. Politics: Who Gets What, When, How. New York: Meridian Books.

Listowel, J. 1968. *The Making of Tanganyika.* London: Chatto & Windus. Second Edition.

Lucas, J. O. 1948. *The Religion of the Yorubas.* Lagos: C. M. S Press.

Lyons, J. 1968. *Introduction to Theoretical Linguistics.* London: Cambridge University Press.

Marcum, J. A. 1988. Black Education in South Africa: Key or Chimera? In H. Kitchen (ed.), *South Africa in Transition to What?* New York: Praeger and The Center for Strategic and International Studies, Washington, D.C.

Marcuse, H. 1968. *One Dimensional Man.* London: Routledge & Kegan Paul.

_____1969. *An Essay on Liberation.* New York: Bacon Press.

Mazrui, A. 1974. *The Political Sociology of the English Language: An African Perspective.* The Hague: Mouton.

_____1976. *A World Federation of Cultures: An African Perspective.* New York: The Free Press.

_____1978. *Political Values and the Educated Class in Africa.* London: Heinemann.

_____1980. *The African Condition*. London: Cambridge University Press.

McCrum, R., W. Cran, and R. MacNeil. 1986. *The Story of English*. New York: Viking Penguin Inc.

Montgomery, M. 1974. *Effective English*. London: Evans Brothers Ltd.

Montgomery M. (with J. O. Bisong and R. E. Morakinyo). 1976-1979. *Effective English*. London: Evans Brothers Ltd.

Moodie, T. D. 1975. *The Rise of Afrikanerdom. Power, Apartheid, and the Afrikaner Civil Religion*. Berkeley: University of California Press.

Mueller, C. 1973. *The Politics of Communication*. New York: Oxford University Press.

Mugomba, A. T., and M. Nyaggah (eds.). 1980. *Independence Without Freedom: The Political Economy of Colonial Education in Southern Africa*. Santa Barbara: ABC-CLIO.

Naipaul, S. 1979. *North of South*. New York: Penguin Books.

National Archives, Ibadan, Nigeria. *Document Number CSO 26/16303*: Use of the Vernacular in Education.

_____*Document Number CSO 26/23889*: Memoranda on the Development of Mission Middle Schools.

_____*Document Numbers CSO 1/1; CSO 1/2; CSO 1/10; and CSO 1/11*: Despatches of the Administrator of Lagos to and from the Governor of the Gold Coast.

Nduka, O. 1964. *Western Education and the Nigerian Cultural Background*. Ibadan: Ibadan University Press.

Newitt, M. 1987. *Portugal in Africa*. London: Hurst.

Ngugi wa Thiong'o. 1986. *Decolonising the Mind: The Politics of Language in African Literature*. London: Heinemann.

Niebuhr, R. 1933. *Moral Man and Immoral Society*. London: Charles Scribner's Sons.

Nigeria, The Federal Republic of. 1989. *Constitution of the Federal Republic of Nigeria*. Lagos: The Federal Government Printer.

_____1981. *National Policy on Education*. Yaba, Lagos: NERC Press.

_____1988. *Cultural Policy for Nigeria*. Lagos: The Federal Government Printer.

Nilsen, A. P. 1973. Sexism in English: A Feminist View. In N. Hoffman et al (eds.), *Female Studies VI: Closer to the Ground*. New York: The Feminist

Press.

Nnoli, O. 1979. Education and Ethnic Politics in Nigeria. In V. C. Uchendu (ed.), *Education and Politics in Tropical Africa*. New York: Conch Magazine Ltd. (Publishers).

Nodolo, I. S. 1989. The Case for Promoting the Nigerian Pidgin Language. *Journal of Modern African Studies* 27: 679-84.

Nohmle (a.k.a. Chisolm, F.). 1992. Teacher lights way to a Xhosa new SA. *The Cape Times*, March 13, 1992: 8.

Nwoye, O. 1978. Language Planning in Nigeria. Ph.D. Dissertation, Georgetown University. University Microfilms: 7913988.

Nyerere, J. K. 1967b. *Education and Self-Reliance*. Dar es Salaam: Government Printer.

O'Barr, J. F. 1976. Language and Politics in Tanzanian Governmental Institutions. In W. M. O'Barr and J. F. O'Barr (eds.), *Language and Politics*, 69-84.

O'Barr, W. M. 1971. Multilingualism in a Rural Tanzanian Village. *Anthropological Linguistics* 13: 289-300.

_____1976. The Study of Language and Politics. In W. M. O'Barr and J. F. O'Barr (eds.), *Language and Politics*, 1-27.

_____1976. Language and Politics in a Rural Tanzanian Council. In W. M. O'Barr and J. F. O'Barr (eds.), *Language and Politics*, 117-133.

Oberprieler, G. 1992. The Language Struggle--Some Thoughts of Language Policy in South Africa. *SASH* 34 (3): 30.

Obiechina, E. 1972. *Onitsha Market Literature*. Ibadan: Heinemann Educational Books.

Ogundipe, P. A. and P. S. Tregidgo. 1971-1975. *Practical English*. London: Longman Group.

Ohmann, R. 1976. *English in America*. New York: Oxford University Press.

Okafo, A. 1985. Lest We Forget. *Sunday Times* (Lagos), June 9.

Oladeji, N. 1987. Women in the Nigerian Novel: Two Novelists. *Lagos Review of English Studies* IX: 116-126.

Omolewa, M. 1975. The English Language in Nigeria, 1862-1960. *Journal of the Nigerian English Studies Association* 7(1&2): 103-117.

_____1985. On the Partition of Modern European Languages in Africa. Paper read at the 30th Congress of the Historical Society of Nigeria, University of Nigeria, Nsukka, 1985.

Osoba, S. O., and A. Fajana. 1980. Educational and Social Developments. In Ikime (ed.), *Groundwork of Nigerian History*, 570-600.

Oyelaran, O. O. 1988. Language, Marginalization and National Development in Nigeria. *Ife Studies in English Language* 2(1): 1-14.

_____1991. Language in Nigeria Towards the Year 2000. In J. - J. Symoens and J. Vanderlinden (eds.), *Les Langues en Afrique a L'Horizon 2000 Symposium*. Brussel: Institut Africain et Academie Royale des Sciences d'Outre-Mer: 109-139.

Paden, J. N. 1968. Language Problems of National Integration in Nigeria: The Special Position of Hausa. In J. A. Fishman, C. A. Ferguson, and J. Das Gupta (eds.), *Language Problems of Developing Nations*, New York: John Wiley and Sons, 199-213.

Parrinder, G. 1953. *Religion in an African City*. London: Oxford University Press.

Paxton, J. 1989. Nigeria. In *The Statesman's Yearbook,* 126th Edition. New York: St. Martin's Press: 941-947.

Pay, B. C. *African Religions*. Englewood Cliffs: Prentice-Hall.

Penelope, J. 1990. *Speaking Freely*. New York: Pergamon Press.

Ploeg, Vander. A. J. 1977. Education in Colonial Africa: The German Experience. *Comparative Education Review* 21(1): 91-109.

Polomé, E. C. 1980. Tanzania: A Socio-Linguistic Perspective. In Polomé and Hill (eds.), *Language in Tanzania,* 103-38.

Roberge, P. T. 1990. The Ideological Profile of Afrikaans Historical Linguistics. In J. E. Joseph and T. J. Taylor (eds.), *Ideologies of Language*, 131-149.

Rodney, W. 1974. *How Europe Underdeveloped Africa*. Washington, D.C.: Howard University Press.

Rommetveit, R. 1968. *Words, Meanings, Messages*. New York: Academic Press and Oslo: Universitetsforlaget.

_____1972b. Deep Structure of Sentences versus Message Structure: Some Critical Remarks to Current Paradigms, and Suggestions for an Alternative Approach. *Norwegian Journal of Linguistics* 26: 3-22.

Rotberg, R. T. (ed.). 1970. *Africa and Its Explorers*. Cambridge: Cambridge University Press.

Ryder, A. F. C. 1969. *Benin and the Europeans 1485-1897*. London: Oxford

University Press.

Sapir, E. 1931. Conceptual Categories in Primitive Languages. *Science* 74 [Reprinted in D. Hymes (ed.), *Language in Culture and Society: A Reader in Linguistics and Anthropology*, New York: Harper and Row, 1964].

_____1949. *Selected Writings in Language, Culture and Personality*, (ed.), D. G. Mandelbaum (ed.), Berkeley: University of California Press.

Saussure, F. de. 1974. *Course in General Linguistics*. Tr. W. Baskin. Glasgow: Collins.

Schleiermacher, F. 1928. *The Christian Faith* Tr. H. L. Mackintosh and J. S. Stewart. Edinburgh: Clark.

Scott, H. S. 1980. *Education Policy in the British Colonial Empire*. London: Evans Brothers Limited.

Scotton, C. M. 1972. *Choosing a Lingua Franca in an African Capital*. Edmonton: Linguistic Research.

_____1990. Elite Closure as Boundary Maintenance. In B. Weinstein (ed.), *Language Policy and Political Development*, Norwood, N. J.: Ablex, 25-42.

Senghor, L. S. 1963. Negritude and the Concept of Universal Civilization. *Presence Africaine* 18.

Sidhom, S. 1969. The Theological Estimate of Man. In K. Dickson and P. Ellingworth (eds.), *Biblical Revelation and African Beliefs*, New York: Orbis Books: 83-115.

Sirles, C. A. 1985. An Evaluative Procedure for Language Planning; The Case of Morocco. Unpublished Ph.D. Dissertation, Northwestern University.

Sofunke, B. 1990. National Language Policy for Democratic Nigeria. In Emenanjo (ed.), *Multilingualism, Minority Languages and Language Policy in Nigeria*, 31-49.

Stageman, B. 1974. The Divorce Dilemma: The New Woman in Contemporary African Novels. *Critique: Studies in Modern Fiction* 15 (3): 90-2.

Sumner, D. L. 1963. *Education in Sierra Leone*. Freetown: Government of Sierra Leone.

Taddese, A. T. 1970. Amharic as a Medium of Instruction in Primary Schools. Paper presented to the Language Association of Eastern Africa, Conference on Language and Development, Nairobi.

Tamuno, T. N. *The Evolution of the Nigerian State: The Southern Phase, 1898-1912*. London: Longman.

Thompson, J. B. 1991. Editor's Introduction. In Bourdieu, *Language and Symbolic Power*, 1-34.

Tordoff, W. 1967. *Government and Politics in Tanzania*. Nairobi: East Africa Publishing House.

Treffgarne, C. 1986. Language Policy in Francophone Africa: Scapegoat or Panacea? In *Language in Education in Africa*, Center for African Studies, Published Seminar Proceedings. Edinburgh: Edinburgh University Press.

Usman, Y. B. 1974. Myths and Mystification in Western Science. *Theory and Practice: Journal of the Nigerian Academy of Arts, Science and Technology* 1: 6-27.

Valkhoff, M. F. 1971. Descriptive Bibliography of the Linguistics of Afrikaans: A Survey of Major Works and Authors. In T. Sebeok (ed.) *Current Trends in Linguistics* 9. The Hague and Paris: Mouton.: 455-500.

Whiteley, W. 1969. *Swahili: The Rise of a National Language*. London: Methuen.

Whorf, B. L. 1956. *Language, Thought, and Reality*, Edited and introduced by J. B. Carroll. Cambridge, Mass.: MIT Press.

Yanga, T. 1980. A Sociolinguistic Identification of Lingala. Unpublished Ph.D. Dissertation, University of Texas, Austin.

INDEX

AFRICAN STUDIES

1. Karla Poewe, **The Namibian Herero: A History of Their Psychosocial Disintegration and Survival**

2. Sara Joan Talis (ed. and trans.), **Oral Histories of Three Secondary School Students in Tanzania**

3. Randolph Stakeman, **The Cultural Politics of Religious Change: A Study of the Sanoyea Kpelle in Liberia**

4. Ayyoub-Awaga Bushara Gafour, **My Father the Spirit-Priest: Religion and Social Organization in the Amaa Tribe (Southwestern Sudan)**

5. Rosalind I. J. Hackett (ed.), **New Religious Movements in Nigeria**

6. Irving Hexham, **Texts on Zulu Religion: Traditional Zulu Ideas About God**

7. Alexandre Kimenyi, **Kinyarwanda and Kirundi Names: A Semio-linguistic Analysis of Bantu Onomastics**

8. G. C. Oosthuizen, (*et al*), **Afro-Christian Religion and Healing in Southern Africa**

9. Karla Poewe, **Religion, Kinship, and Economy in Luapula, Zambia**

10. Mario Azevedo (ed.), **Cameroon and Chad in Historical and Contemporary Perspectives**

11. John E. Eberegbulam Njoku, **Traditionalism Versus Modernism at Death: Allegorical Tales of Africa**

12. David Hirschmann, **Changing Attitudes of Black South Africans Toward the United States**

13. Panos Bardis, **South Africa and the Marxist Movement: A Study in Double Standards**

14. John E. Eberegbulam Njoku, **The Igbos of Nigeria: Ancient Rites, Changes and Survival**

15. W. Alade Fawole, **Military Interventions in Nigerian Politics, 1966-1985: Toward Alternative Explanations**

16. Kenoye Kelvin Eke, **Nigeria's Foreign Policy Under Two Military Governments, 1966-1979: An Analysis of the Gowan and Muhammed/Obasanjo Regimes**

17. Herbert Ekwe-Ekwe, **The Biafra War: Nigeria and the Aftermath**

18. I. D. Talbott, **Agricultural Innovation in Colonial Africa: Kenya and the Great Depression**

29. G. C. Oosthuizen and Irving Hexham (eds.), **Afro-Christian Religion at the Grassroots in Southern Africa**

20. Bessie House-Midamba, **Class Development and Gender Inequality in Kenya, 1963-1990**